GCSE Business Studies

PASS PLUS

for AQA

Edited by Neil Denby

+ Peter Kennerdell
+ Alan Williams
+ Mike Schofield

Hodder & Stoughton

A MEMBER OF THE HODDER HEADLINE GROUP

Orders: please contact Bookpoint Ltd, 130 Milton Park, Abingdon, Oxon OX14 4SB. Telephone: (44) 01235 827720.
Fax: (44) 01235 400454. Lines are open from 9.00 – 6.00, Monday to Saturday, with a 24 hour message answering service.
You can also order through our website www.hodderheadline.co.uk.

British Library Cataloguing in Publication Data
A catalogue record for this title is available from the British Library

ISBN 0 340 87674 3

First Published 2003
Impression number   10 9 8 7 6 5 4 3 2 1
Year   2007 2006 2005 2004 2003

Typeset by Pantek Arts Ltd.
Printed in Spain for Hodder & Stoughton Educational, a division of Hodder Headline Plc, 338 Euston Road, London, NW1 3BH.

CONTENTS

PREFACE

This resource has been written specifically to help candidates improve their chances of achieving a higher grade at GCSE Business Studies. It has been developed in such a way to allow teachers to use it with their students or, to allow students to work through the material independently. It was never our intention to provide a highly visual resource which is light on substance and does not allow access to higher grades. Candidates should be able to either 'dip into' the resource to improve understanding of certain topics, or work through the whole of it at the end of their course as they prepare for their examinations.

The resource has been designed to be used in conjunction with existing GCSE course books and the notes which students will have accumulated during their course. It is not intended to be a course book but a resource which provides 'triggers', such as those found in the **Revision Activity**, to help remind students about what they have learned and how this information may be used in different contexts. The **Putting it into Context** section will provide an opportunity for students to see how their knowledge and understanding of a particular topic can be set within a particular context, similar to some of the scenarios used in examination papers.

Candidates will be preparing for one of two AQA specifications; Specification A or Specification B. These specifications share common content (as do all GCSE Business Studies examinations) but have different approaches and methods of assessment. Examples are drawn from both specifications. It is important that candidates are aware of which specification they are following.

The activities we have included have been designed to help reinforce learning and preparation for the final examination. In some cases, these activities will take a very different approach to those which students have probably experienced in class. In other cases, the activities may be very similar. The **Introduction** gives further information on preparation for the final examination.

The contents of this resource are also based on our collective experience as examiners and teachers of GCSE Business Studies. Detailed information is provided on the **question types** which candidates should expect to find in the examination papers dealing with the main specification content of AQA GCSE Business Studies.

We have also tried to provide an insight into the high quality answers and the problems, mistakes and misunderstandings which candidates often make in examinations, by including **student answers** to examination type questions. Student responses to questions are based on answers written by students but selected and adapted to illustrate particular points. Higher Tier examination questions are targeted primarily at grades A* to B whilst common questions are targeted at grades C and D. We have deliberately avoided including a large number of knowledge recall type questions.

What the Examiner Says gives information on what the examiner may be looking for in answer to a question. It must be remembered that the questions are targeted at the **higher end of the ability range for GCSE**. We have done this deliberately, for the purpose of this book is to help candidates achieve higher grades and therefore there would be little point in not having high expectations of candidate answers. Candidate names do not refer to any one particular candidate but have been included to add an element of reality and improve readability.

In the **Case Study** section, we have provided a stimulus and some guidance on how students might use stimulus material to prepare for the examination. One of the distinctions between AQA Specification A and AQA Specification B is that the A course uses a pre-seen Case Study used as stimulus material. Students should be able to see from the information how questions can be developed from stimulus material which can be taken as an alternative to coursework. There is little point in having a pre-seen Case Study without doing some preparation by considering the types of questions which may be asked. The **Examination Questions** section is split into the main areas of study of a GCSE Business Studies course. Students will be able to choose Higher Tier type questions on a topic-by-topic basis. We have, though, included some Foundation Tier questions for extra practice.

Finally some thanks. Firstly to Colin Goodlad of Hodder Arnold in helping with the preparation of the material. Secondly to the many thousands of candidates whom we have both taught and examined over the years who have given us the ideas for this resource. We wish we could have been able to help you! Finally, to our families who have, once again been very patient and understanding whilst we completed the task.

We hope you find the resource helps with your examination preparation. Good luck!

PART ONE

INTRODUCTION – PREPARING FOR THE EXAMINATION

This chapter is to help you prepare for the examinations that you will sit in Business Studies. Your assessment is likely to be a combination of examination work and coursework. No advice on coursework is given in this book. There is detailed guidance for coursework, further examples of examination questions and a more in-depth treatment of subject matter in the books *GCSE Business Studies for AQA Specification A* (Jenkins and Hamman, ISBN 0 340 77268 9) and *GCSE Business Studies for AQA Specification B* (Denby and Thomas, ISBN 0 340 80116 6). You may also find the *Business Studies Workbook* (Denby and Thomas, ISBN 0 340 77232 8) useful. All of these are published by Hodder & Stoughton Educational.

The Examination

It is the job of an examiner who writes a GCSE paper to set questions that give the candidate the opportunity to show what they know, understand and can do. The examiner is not trying to set trick questions! You can be confident that if you have prepared yourself properly, you will get the result that you deserve.

Preparation will lead to success

AQA Business Studies Examinations involve a number of questions that will be set around one or more real or realistic business situations. The four 'assessment objectives' tested can be summarised under the headings of knowledge, application, analysis and evaluation. In Specification A the questions are based on a Case Study, which Candidates receive in advance of the examination. There are two sections. Section A principally tests the Assessment Objectives of **knowledge** and **application**. Section B mainly tests **analysis** and **evaluation**.

In Specification B there are three possible papers to take. Paper 1 has questions, testing all assessment objectives, asked in the context of an unseen Case Study, usually a 'story' of business being established, growing and facing problems, which runs through the paper. Paper 2 is a paper that can be taken as an alternative to coursework, and is dealt with separately in the Case Study section. Paper 3 uses a number of smaller business situations on which to base its questions. Words in the questions, called **command words**, will help you to know what skill is being tested. It is worth knowing a little about assessment objectives and command words – it will help you to write high scoring answers. The assessment objectives are explained in the boxes below:

Knowledge This is about the meaning of terms and ideas. Typical command words that indicate knowledge questions are *list*, *state* and *explain*. For example:

- State the 4Ps connected with marketing.
- Explain the meaning of the term marketing.

Application This skill is about using knowledge or skills to discuss or calculate something about the business in the examination paper. *Explain* is a typical command word – but in this type of question you will be asked to explain how something affects the business in the examination paper. Calculate is another common command word telling you to apply your numeracy skills. Example questions are:

- Explain how John Taylor, as a sole trader, will be affected by unlimited liability.
- Calculate the percentage mark-up on goods bought in at 15p and sold at 25p.

Analysis This is about using information to discuss or break down a problem – most commonly in Business Studies you need to discuss the advantages and disadvantages of something. You may also be required to interpret data, for example, comparing trends and making predictions (often some form of calculation may be involved). Typical commands in a question may be *compare* or *discuss* or a longer statement such as *explain the advantages and disadvantages* of something. Example questions are:

- Discuss the changes that may have caused the rise in turnover between 1998 and 1999.
- State and explain the benefits and problems that the local council should take into consideration when deciding whether or not to approve planning application for a new airport.

Evaluation This is about making judgements. You may need to decide how well a business has performed or suggest what a business should do. Your judgement will be based on either evidence (data in the question or your own knowledge) or reasoned argument – often a discussion of pros and cons of a course of action. Typical command words are *evaluate* and *recommend*. Example questions are:

- Using the information in the Trading and Profit and Loss Account (and/or Balance Sheet), evaluate the performance of the business in 2002 compared with 2001.
- Recommend whether or not John Taylor should go into partnership or remain as a sole trader.

MULTI-SKILL QUESTIONS

In practice, to answer most questions successfully, you need to use more than one of the four skills. Evaluation questions usually need you to apply your knowledge to give an analysis of a problem before making a judgement.

MARK SCHEMES

Questions are almost always marked using a 'levels of response' mark scheme, this means that they are marked on the whole answer, and that lists and short answers do not score very highly. This means that you can earn marks by giving a better quality answer (not a longer one) by moving into the higher order examination skills such as analysis, synthesis and evaluation. Look at the following question:

Question Jason Lee is leaving Colliers PLC (a chocolate manufacturer and retailer) and intends to open a shop selling chocolates and sweets. Should he open a shop as a franchise or as an independent shop? Discuss the advantages and disadvantages of each option to give reasons for your answer.

Mark Scheme

Level One ● The candidate describes the advantages of both options – either opening as a franchise or as an independent trader.

Level Two ● The candidate discusses the advantages/disadvantages of both options.

Level Three ● The candidate comes to a conclusion and gives a reason for the decision.

At Level 1, the Candidate is demonstrating knowledge. However much is written about each alternative, it is not possible to reach the next level without comparing the two (this is analysis).

At Level 2, the comparison is made (an analysis such as; on the one hand... on the other hand...).

At Level 3, the Candidate is showing skills of synthesis – drawing the threads of an argument together, and reasoned judgement, coming to a conclusion. So you can see that it is important to write a quality answer!

WRITING FRAMES

A neat way to make sure that you write good answers to analysis and evaluation questions is to use writing frames like the one below.

Advantages/Strengths/ Arguments for	Disadvantages/Weaknesses/ Arguments against

Reasons for conclusion/decision/recommendation

For example, a writing frame for the question marked using a levels of response mark scheme given above would be:

Arguments for opening as a franchise	**Arguments against opening as a franchise**
• Tried and tested product • Support/advice from franchiser • Advertising undertaken by franchiser	• Royalty must be paid to franchiser • Owner does not have total control • Must buy stock from franchiser

Reasons for conclusion/decision/recommendation

Open as an independent – Jason has worked in chocolate business so has knowledge/skills necessary to succeed.
OR
Open as a franchise – more chance of success, the majority of small, independent businesses do not last more than 12 months.

SO WHAT? OR CONSEQUENCE DIAGRAMS

These are another useful way to get your ideas together to answer a question. Businesses are affected by all kinds of changes. A 'So What?' or 'Consequence' diagram shows the sequence of changes that may take place after something is altered. The following is an example of a question that asks you to say what will happen to the business as a result of a change:

Question Explain how a rise in interest rates will affect XYZ Ltd

CONSEQUENCE DIAGRAM:

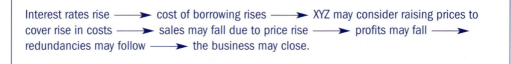

Interest rates rise ⟶ cost of borrowing rises ⟶ XYZ may consider raising prices to cover rise in costs ⟶ sales may fall due to price rise ⟶ profits may fall ⟶ redundancies may follow ⟶ the business may close.

In this example, the business may be affected in another way – a second Consequence Diagram is needed.

Interest rates rise ⟶ consumers have less disposable income ⟶ demand falls (for certain goods) ⟶ sales fall due to fall in demand ⟶ and so on down to the business folding.

These consequence diagrams help you to learn to explain fully sequences of events. This can help you to score high marks.

Revising for the Examination

SECTION 2

There will be a lot to revise for a Business Studies GCSE examination. This section explains some useful techniques for revision and gives some advice about planning a revision programme.

BEFORE YOU START

Make sure that the room you use is organised. You should work at a desk and in good light – natural or electric. Have paper, pens, rulers, rubbers and so on to hand. If you want to listen to music do so – but you should not listen to a radio programme with a DJ who may become a distraction. The best music to listen to is instrumental music – perhaps this is the time to get into classical music! Have regular breaks when you walk around, have a drink or something to eat. Do not make these breaks too frequent – you should be able to work for at least 30 minutes without one.

TECHNIQUES OF REVISION

Very few people are able to read something and then remember it in detail. Revising is hard work. It is best done by being active – by writing or drawing or creating something. There is no single way to revise. We all have different styles of learning – some like to make notes, others like images such as pictures and diagrams, others like to be physically active. You should choose revision techniques that suit your learning style. Different parts of Business Studies suit different revision techniques. You should also use different techniques so that there is some variety in your work. The following are some useful revision techniques.

KNOWLEDGE HIERARCHIES OR SUMMARY LISTS

Long sets of notes can be difficult to learn. Summarising them into a list of key words is fantastically helpful. Columns are used to organise the words into a 'hierarchy' – the most important terms go to the left of the page in the first column, lesser terms in the next columns.

As well as the example that follows, there are further examples throughout this book. Note that a knowledge hierarchy is different from brainstorming – with hierarchies the information is organised and classified into groups. They need to be neat – it helps to create a 'picture' that you will remember in the exam.

The following summarises the important terms related to the 4Ps of marketing.

The Marketing Mix

Topic	Key Features	Detail	Further Information
Product	• Customer wants • Product range/mix	• Design • Features • Job	• Size, colour
Price	• Competition-based	• Higher • Lower • Same	• Exclusive • Switch customer to you • Distinguish by using a different form of competition
	• Penetration price	• Low then raise price	• Gain market share
	• Creaming/Skimming	• High then lower price	• Make profit, then increase sales
	• Cost plus pricing	• Add profit margin	• Depends on what customers will pay
Place	• Direct to customer	• Vending machine • Mail order • Internet • Farmer's roadside stall	
	or • Through wholesaler/retailer	• Shop	
Promotion	• Advertising	• Direct or • Indirect • Persuasive or • Informative	• To specific individuals • To anyone watching • Often plays on emotions • Gives factual details
	• Sales Promotions	• Buy one get one free • Added value • Price reductions • Loss leaders • Competitions • Free samples • Merchandising • After-sales service	

You will find another, slightly different version of this list in the unit about Marketing. There is no 'right' or 'wrong' list. **The list that you will remember is the one that you draw up yourself.** You are strongly advised to try to create your own and, then, perhaps compare it with the one in the book. You will remember much more from creating your own than from reading an example. To create one you should go through the notes that your teacher has given to you or through a chapter in a textbook.

You will find that creating the list helps you to remember. The next time you revise marketing you may only need to learn the first two columns – they will 'trigger off' all the other points. When you know it well enough, you will only need to remember the first four words – product, price, place and promotion – and these will remind you of everything else.

MIND MAPS OR STAR DIAGRAMS

These do a similar job to summary lists. Some people, particularly those who like visual things (diagrams, pictures), find mind maps more useful than lists. The following mind map summarises some key points about introducing technology into production in manufacturing industry. Like knowledge hierarchies, the information in a mind map should be organised logically.

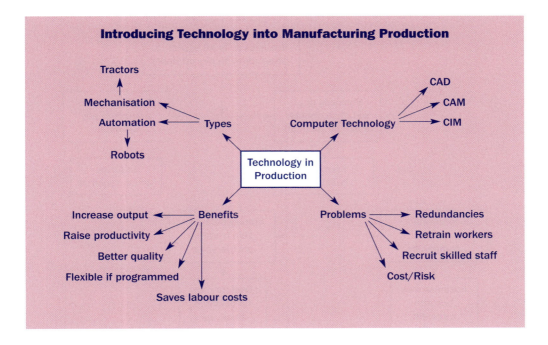

Introducing Technology into Manufacturing Production

FLOW CHARTS

These are useful for summarising a chain or sequence of events that might happen. The following may help to revise the difference between unlimited and limited liability.

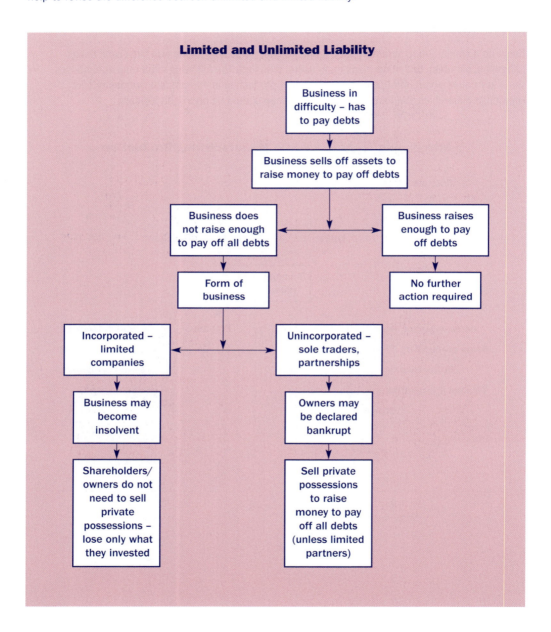

Limited and Unlimited Liability

Business in difficulty – has to pay debts

Business sells off assets to raise money to pay off debts

Business does not raise enough to pay off all debts

Business raises enough to pay off debts

Form of business

No further action required

Incorporated – limited companies

Unincorporated – sole traders, partnerships

Business may become insolvent

Owners may be declared bankrupt

Shareholders/ owners do not need to sell private possessions – lose only what they invested

Sell private possessions to raise money to pay off all debts (unless limited partners)

IMAGE CHAINS

Like flow charts, these are useful for learning sequences of events. Instead of boxes with words in them, they use boxes with pictures or cartoons. The following image chain shows the sequence of events for recruiting and selecting a new worker.

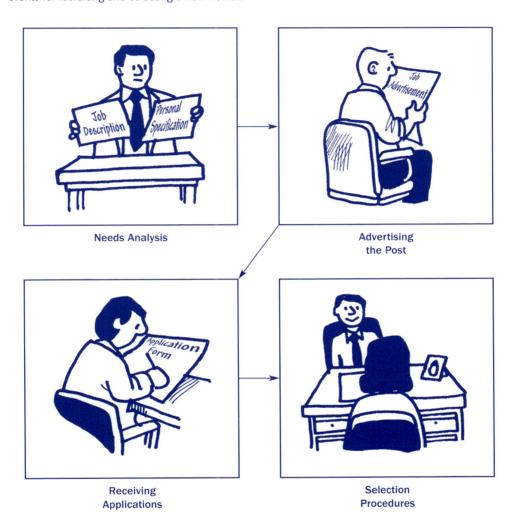

Needs Analysis

Advertising the Post

Receiving Applications

Selection Procedures

PICTURES

Labelling a picture with key words is another technique. The following is a reminder of what a person specification is and the sources of information the employer can use to tell if the person meets the specification.

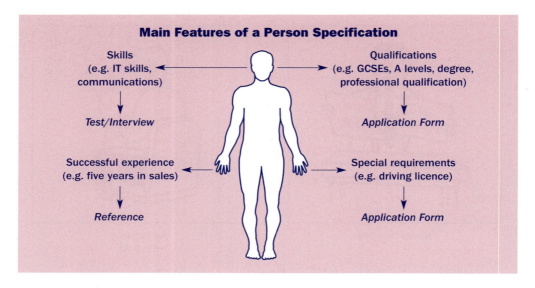

WORD ASSOCIATIONS

An alternative to a diagram is word association. Link a key term with another term to help you to remember. For example, to help to remember the points about person specifications, you might link the key words as follows:

- My big brain = qualifications
- The teacher's grey hair = experience
- Hands = skills
- My big nose = special requirements.

POEMS, RAPS AND (SILLY) STORIES

Students who are creative or are musical often like poems, raps or silly stories. They are good for learning a list of terms. The poem, rap or story should include all the terms that you need to learn. These do not need to be very good – it is writing them that is useful. The sillier they are the more you will remember them. The rhyme opposite reminds you how to draw the graph of the product life cycle, of its stages, and of what happens at each of those stages.

Couplets for the product life cycle.

As a **product** I can say, over time I've had my day,

Sales on left and **time** below let me know how I should grow.

I was born in **research** land, **launched** when I'm complete

Grew so big that other firms started to compete

So my sales began to fall when I reached **maturity**

Competitors took market share – folk bought them instead of me!

Soon everyone had one of me, a second or a third

With many versions out there, **saturation** was the word

At the last I'd had my day, and moved into **decline**

Lost the will to live, and went finally to **die**.

(I could have had a second life, by changing bits of me, if my firm had seen to use an **extension strategy**.)

Planning Revision

PLANNING YOUR REVISION

The average person needs to revise things three or four times. When we learn something for the first time, we will forget 80% of it within 24 hours. Each time you revise, more of what you learn stays firmly in the memory.

You will find it useful to make a plan. This will help you to organise yourself so that you get things done and make progress. Follow the steps suggested below. You might do this planning once every month in the period leading up to the examination.

Step One: Self-Review

This will help you to think about what you need to concentrate on in order to improve your work. You write down what you are confident about in your studies and those things that you think are your main weaknesses. Use the self-review sheet on page 14. Alternatively, your teacher may have given you lists of things to know about each topic in Business Studies. Tick and cross items on the list depending on how well you feel you know them. If not, your teacher can get lists from AQA (they are in the published schemes of work or in your text book). It will boost your confidence each time you review a topic – you should have become confident about more things.

Step Two: Study Timetable

This is your weekly plan. This is really important for helping you 'to make things happen'. You need to write down exactly what you will do each day for your revision – you should write SMART targets (see Setting Revision Targets on page 15). You could use the weekly planner on page 16.

Step Three: Make it Happen

Carry out your weekly plan. You will find it useful to write down any work that you find difficult – seek help perhaps from your teacher to overcome the problem.

Step Four: Self-Review

At the end of the month, complete another self-review. Write more plans for the next month's work.

SELF-REVIEW: STRENGTHS AND WEAKNESSES

The purpose of this sheet to help you to think about what topics you need to work on to improve. In the 'Strengths' column, for each topic, write down three things that you think you have done or know well. In the 'Weaknesses' column, write down three things you need to improve.

Topic	Strengths	Weaknesses
External environment of business	1 2 3	1 2 3
Business structure and organisation	1 2 3	1 2 3
Marketing	1 2 3	1 2 3
Production	1 2 3	1 2 3
Finance	1 2 3	1 2 3
People in organisations	1 2 3	1 2 3
Aiding and controlling business activity	1 2 3	1 2 3
Option (Marketing or Business and change)	1 2 3	1 2 3

SETTING REVISION TARGETS

Targets that you set should be SMART.

Use these questions to check that you write SMART targets.

Specific
Do my targets say exactly what I need to do?

Measureable
How will I be able to prove that I have met my targets?

Achievable
Will I be able to achieve my target in the time?

Realistic
Are my targets about action that I can take?

Time-related
Have I set deadlines for meeting my targets?

SMART targets are:

Specific

Measureable

Achievable

Realistic

Time-related

Revision Targets – are these targets SMART?

Which of these targets do you think are SMART?

- I will revise my Business Studies.
- I will make notes on economies of scale.
- I will learn 20 terms connected with the Marketing by Thursday.
- Tonight I will write a revision action plan for next week.
- I will read notes on Production Techniques.
- I will write a rap about ratios used to analyse balance sheets tonight.

STUDY TIMETABLE

For the week beginning _____ Name _____

Times	Monday	Tuesday	Wednesday	Thursday	Friday	Times	Saturday	Sunday
Morning	School	School	School	School	School	9 – 10		
Afternoon	School	School	School	School	School	10 – 11		
4.15 – 5.00						11 – 12		
5.00 – 5.30						12 – 1		
5.30 – 6.30						1 – 2		
6.30 – 7.00						3 – 4		
7.00 – 7.30						4 – 6		
7.30 – 8.00						6 – 7		
8.00 – 8.30						7 – 8		
8.30 – 9.00						8 – 9		

In the Examination

SECTION 4

If you have revised thoroughly, you can be confident about sitting the examination. Remember, it is the job of the examiner who writes the paper to set a paper that tests what you know, understand and can do – not to try to catch you out with trick questions. The following rules may help you to do justice to your ability.

- Make sure that you go into the examination with all the equipment that you need – pens, pencils, rulers, rubbers and a calculator.
- At the beginning of the examination take your time – do not panic and rush your work.
- Read the questions carefully. Make sure that you understand what the question is asking you to do.
- Obey any specific instructions such as 'Show your working' or 'State and explain TWO...'.
- Develop fully the points you wish to make.
- Use the specialist Business Studies terms that you have learnt.
- Remember that writing frames can help for longer, analysis and evaluation questions.
- Write neatly.
- Take care when drawing diagrams – be sure to label them.
- Write clearly – remember that some questions have additional marks for the Quality of Written Communications.
- Answer ALL the questions as instructed.

Using this Book

In Part Two of the book, each section deals with a specific part of the AQA GCSE Business Studies Specification. Each section is divided into the following sub-sections.

SOME BASICS

This is intended to remind you briefly of the main areas of the topic – very little detail is given here. The aim is to see how the different areas fit together within the topic.

Revision Material

KNOWLEDGE HIERARCHIES OR SUMMARY LISTS

These provide you with main terms that are connected with the topic. Working to the right, each column provides additional detail. Learning these is very useful. Better still, use your notes and your Business Studies textbook to create your own knowledge hierarchy – it is not easy but you can be sure you will remember more from doing this compared with reading the one in the book. Compare the one you make with the one in the book.

PUTTING IT IN CONTEXT

This sub-section shows how the main ideas can be applied to business situations to explain, analyse or evaluate them. For candidates who want to perform at the highest level, knowing how to apply your knowledge in this way is vital. You are recommended to read over the section before attempting any relevant question(s).

ACTIVITIES

These are short activities that you may find useful to check your understanding before dealing with longer, examination type questions. Additionally or instead, you might want to use some of the revision techniques suggested earlier in this Introduction to make absolutely sure that you are completely familiar with the topic.

You will find a list of question types connected with the content of the section varying from (usually straightforward) knowledge type questions to the more difficult analysis and evaluation question types.

Specimen Questions

In this sub-section you will find a range of higher (A–B) and common (C–D) questions covering the topic. You will also find an answer that has been written by a student and some comments by an examiner about this answer. The answers are not all perfect. It can be useful to read perfect answers. Equally, it can be useful to read answers that are not so good and then read the examiner's explanation about how the answer could have been improved – learning from mistakes is one of the best ways of learning.

One of the main failings of many candidates in examinations is that they do not use their knowledge fully to answer the questions that are set. Making use of the Specimen Questions should help you to avoid this. Above all you are recommended to use one or more of the following approaches to the Specimen Questions.

- Write an answer to the questions and then compare your answer with the student's answer and the comments from the examiner.
- Write notes, perhaps using a writing frame or consequence diagram, instead of a full written answer and then compare what you have written with the student's answer and the examiner's comments.
- Read the student's answer to a question and then try to write a better answer, using the advice from the examiner.

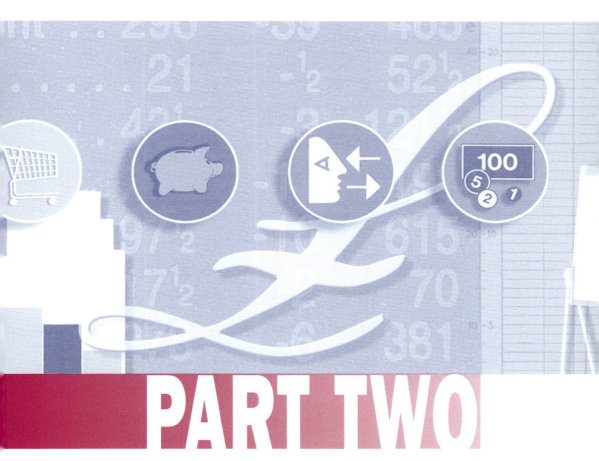

2

PART TWO

REVISING BUSINESS STUDIES

The Knowledge Hierarchies and the Activities in each of the units of this section should help students to recall the knowledge content of Business Studies. Primarily, though, this section is about the application of knowledge to analyse and evaluate business contexts. This is demonstrated in the Putting it in Context sections while the Questions Types to Expect, Student Answers and What the Examiner Says are designed to show how knowledge may be applied in the examination situation.

The External Environment of Business

SECTION 1

SOME BASICS

Organisations produce goods and services. Some are privately owned businesses and exist in the private sector of the economy, others are organisations owned by the state or government and exist in the public sector. They use resources (land, labour, capital and enterprise or organisation). Consumer goods satisfy consumer wants, capital goods are sold to businesses and public organisations to help them to produce more goods and services. Organisations usually set objectives, though these will differ depending on whether they are private or publicly owned.

All organisations can be classified as primary, secondary or tertiary sector organisations, depending on what they provide or produce. The relative importance of the three sectors has changed significantly in the past 100 years.

Stakeholders are people and organisations who are affected by business activity. Some will be affected by the private costs and benefits of the activity, others by the social costs and benefits.

Revision Material

> **KNOWLEDGE HIERARCHY: LIST OF THINGS TO KNOW ABOUT THE EXTERNAL ENVIRONMENT OF BUSINESS**

This information is intended to provide a quick reminder. Your notes, and the information in the textbook you have used, should provide more detailed information and examples.

Topic	Key Features	Detail	Further Information
Economic problem	• Scarcity	• Unlimited wants	• Basic needs • Luxuries
		• Limited resources (factors of production)	• Land • Labour • Capital • Enterprise
	• Choice	• Who, What, Where, How to produce	
	• Opportunity cost	• Sacrifice connected with choice	• Mars or Yorkie bar

Topic	Key Features	Detail	Further Information
Goods and Services	• Consumer goods and services	• Clothing • Food • Houses • Entertainments • Holidays	
	• Capital goods	• Machines • Tools • Offices • Factories	
Sectors of the Economy (1)	• Primary	• Take raw materials from	• Farming • Fishing • Mining • Forestry
	• Secondary	• Manufacturing and construction industry	• Clothing • Building • Processed foods • Electrical goods
	• Tertiary	• Services	• Retailing • Leisure • Financial • Transport • Health
Objectives	• Survival • Profit • Provision of a service • Growth	• Sales • Market Share	
Sectors of the Economy (2)	• Private sector	• Privately owned businesses	• Sole traders • Partnerships • Limited companies • Co-operatives
	• Public organisations	• State/government owned organisations	• Health Service • BBC • Local councils • Police Force • Armed Forces
Stakeholders	• Workers and managers	• Jobs • Income	
	• Owners	• Profits • Capital appreciation	

Topic	Key Features	Detail	Further Information
Stakeholders *cont.*	• Customers	• Goods and services	
	• Suppliers	• Sales	
	• Competitors	• Sales	
	• Government	• Government spending • Taxation	• Social Security • Income tax • VAT
Benefits	• Private	• Income	• Profits • Wages, salaries
	• Social	• Jobs in the community • Spending in the community • Service for community	
Costs	• Private	• Fixed costs	• Rent for factory; shop
		• Variable costs	• Wages • Raw materials • Power
	• Social	• Pollution • Loss of land	• Air, noise, river • Scenery • Leisure facility • Natural habitats
Government	• Local	• Planning permission • Control pollution	
	• National	• Give grants • Laws and regulations	
Pressure Groups	• Business groups	• CBI • Trade Associations	
	• Consumer groups	• Consumer's Association	
	• Environmental groups	• Greenpeace • Friends of the Earth	
	• Worker groups	• Trade Unions • Professional Associations	

PUTTING IT IN CONTEXT

The economy of Moorshire has changed significantly in the past 20 years. Despite increases in the amount produced, employment in both the *primary* and *secondary* sectors continued to fall, with the greatest falls in the secondary sector. The fall is largely due to the increased use of *technology*, especially *computer integrated manufacturing* in secondary industries such as car assembly, chemical production and furniture manufacture. Output might have grown even more in both sectors but for the increase in the amount of raw materials and food and of manufactured goods that are now imported in the UK. Had this happened, employment levels in the primary and secondary sectors might not have fallen.

The *tertiary* sector has experienced rapid growth, both in output and employment. As the income of people in the county has risen, they have more money to spend in shops and on services such as leisure, recreation and tourism. The financial services such as banking, insurance and the savings industries have also grown rapidly. Many people, previously employed in the primary

Examples of businesses in the primary sector

and secondary sectors, have found employment in the tertiary sector, though some too old or too set in their ways have not been prepared to undertake the necessary training to develop the new skills

Example of business in the secondary sector

Examples of businesses in the tertiary sector

needed in the new economy. Overall employment has risen, though more jobs are part-time and workers are expected to be more flexible in the hours they work.

With the closure of the coal mining industry, the Moorshire County Council decided to build an industrial estate to attract new businesses to the area. The industrial estate has been a success, with owners generally reporting good profits. Some other *stakeholders* have been pleased by the *social benefits* that have resulted – the workers who built the new factories, people who work in the new factories, other businesses in Moorshire whose trade has increased because workers generally now have more money to spend and those businesses who supply materials and services to the new firms on the estates. Yet other stakeholders have been concerned about the *social costs* of the developments. Some have objected to the increase in traffic and the air and noise pollution that followed, whilst environmental groups, including the pressure group, Friends of the Earth, have been concerned about the loss of land the natural habitats of some wild animals.

The *objective* of the County Council in providing the industrial estate has been to provide a *service* to the community so that the people who live in it have jobs. The development has also increased the tax income of the Council which has meant that it is able to provide more or better services such as education and social services. Peter Winstanley started a small picture-framing business on the estate. His objective was to develop some regular customers and to make enough profit just to *survive* the first year in business. Catherine Tresor moved her car radio business to new premises on the industrial estate because, after three successful years, she believed she could *expand* the business to include auto electric services. She needed larger premises as well as new employees.

Pressure groups affect business

ACTIVITIES

ACTIVITY ONE
Use the words in the 'Words to use' list to complete the following diagram to explain the basic economic problem.

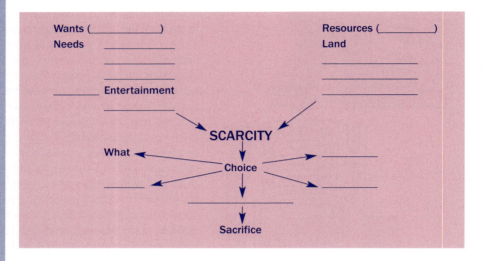

Words to use
Limited, Food, Opportunity, Cost, Where, How, Capital, Shelter, Luxuries, Labour, Who for, Unlimited, TV, Enterprise, Clothing

ACTIVITY TWO
Hurleston Detergents Ltd makes soap and washing powder. It is located in Clevedon. Despite enjoying a 15% market share, the business is no longer profitable and it will be closed down in two months. At present it employs 500 workers. Draw a 'mind map' or 'star diagram' to identify the stakeholders in Hurleston Detergents Ltd and how they will be affected by the closure.

ACTIVITY THREE
Bolton Wanderers Football Club built their stadium, The Reebok, on an area of land, the Red Moss, near the town of Horwich. A shopping centre, the Middlebrook, was developed around the stadium. The Moss was a natural habitat for plant, birds and animals.

Copy and complete the writing frame below to show the likely social benefits and costs of the development. In the lower box, state what other information you would need to decide

Social benefits of The Reebok and Middlebrook	Social costs of The Reebok and Middlebrook

Additional information needed to judge if the development has been good or bad for the local community

whether the development of the Reebok and Middlebrook Shopping Centre had been good or bad for the local community.

ACTIVITY FOUR

Copy and complete the table below. Using your knowledge of business objectives (or those given in the Knowledge Hierarchy), state which ones are likely to be appropriate to each organisation.

	Marks and Spencers plc	A new mobile phone provider – in its first year of trading	Bolton Metropolitan Borough Council
Business Objectives			

ACTIVITY FIVE

Using a 'Yellow Pages' or your own knowledge of the area in which you live, write down three examples of businesses in each of the following sectors of the economy: primary, secondary and tertiary.

QUESTION TYPES TO EXPECT

AQA 'A' questions may ask you to give the meaning and examples of terms such as the following. With AQA 'B', you will still need to know them, but are usually asked to use them in the context of the question:

- *Primary, Secondary and Tertiary Sectors*
- *Opportunity Cost*
- *Wants and Resources (Factors of Production)*
- *Consumer and Capital Goods*
- *Stakeholders*
- *Social Costs and Benefits*

Both specfications may ask more difficult questions such as:

- *Explain why changes in the employment and output in the primary, secondary and tertiary sectors have occurred.*
- *Analyse employment figures to evaluate the effects on a population of a change in employment in different sectors.*
- *Identify stakeholders in a business and explain how they may be affected by changes in its activity such as its closure or expansion.*
- *Identify the objectives that different types of businesses may have.*
- *Identify the social costs and benefits that may result from some kind of business development such as the development of land for commercial use.*
- *Explain how government and pressure groups may influence the external environment of a business.*

Some examples of these types of questions and student answers are given in the following section. Look carefully at what the question is asking you to do; how the student has answered the question; what the examiner thinks of the answer.

EXTERNAL ENVIRONMENT OF BUSINESS: SPECIMEN QUESTIONS

Question One (Common Question)

The table below shows the changes that have taken place in employment in the three sectors of the economy in the County of Wetland during the period 1960 to 2000.

Year	Primary Sector	Secondary Sector	Tertiary Sector
1960	10,000	120,000	180,000
1980	7000	90,000	230.000
2000	5000	70,000	260,000

a) Describe the main changes that have taken place in employment in each sector of the economy in the period 1960 to 2000. **(6)**

b) Explain why the changes in employment in i) the primary sector and ii) the secondary sector may have occurred during the period 1960 to 2000. **(8)**

c) Explain why the changes in employment in the tertiary sector of the economy of Wetland may have occurred during the period 1960 to 2000. **(6)**

Student Answer

a)   During the period 1960 to 2000 the primary sector has fallen as more machinery is being used. As more machines are used, fewer workers are needed. The secondary sector has also fallen as more people are buying from abroad. This is because it is cheaper, technology is more up-to-date and it is more efficient. The tertiary sector has seen a large increase in the numbers of people employed – in percentage terms the rise is nearly 45%.

b) i)   The primary sector has fallen in employment because more machines and better methods of production are now used – this means that a bigger output of goods can be produced from fewer people. Output per person has also increased because of better techniques of production – for example, genetic engineering has increased the amount that can been grown in one field. No extra workers are needed to make this output.

ii)   The secondary sector has seen a fall in employment also partly because of the use of new technologies such as CAD and CAM. For example, car factories now employ fewer people than they used to because robots do a lot of the work. Also, although the demand for manufactured goods has increased, a lot of these goods are bought from abroad because other countries can produce them more cheaply. For example, a lot of clothing and training shoes are made in the Far East because wages are lower there.

c)   The changes in the tertiary sector are caused by a rise in population, meaning that more *teachers and health workers are needed. Also people have more money to spend now because wages have gone up. They can spend this in shops and so more retail workers are needed. People also have more leisure time meaning more leisure parks and centres are being built which requires more workers. Finally, businesses might have placed more importance on customer service as a way of keeping existing customers and gaining new ones. This could lead to a large increase in telephone call centres which themselves need large numbers of workers.*

Kirsty

What the Examiner Says

a) Kirsty has misinterpreted the question to an extent. The command word here is 'describe'. Kirsty does describe the changes – at a very basic level for primary and secondary sectors and at a higher level, using percentages, for the tertiary sector. There was no need to 'explain' the changes – this is required in part b) of the question. To gain more marks, Kirsty could have made some comparative comments to the effect that the biggest decline was in the secondary sector and supported the argument with some figures, either for the total changes in employment or (even better) the percentage changes in employment.

Marks awarded – 4 out of 6

b) Kirsty presents a very good answer here. She states reasons why the level of employment in both primary and secondary sectors may have fallen and then illustrates these with clear, appropriate examples.

Marks awarded – 8 out of 8

c) Kirsty discusses a range of possible reasons why there are more jobs in the tertiary sector. She could have made more of some of the points – for example, the increase in incomes along with the increase in leisure time, have resulted in a greater demand for leisure services. It would also have been worth noting that a lot of these services are labour intensive – machinery cannot often be used instead of labour. Still a good answer!

Marks awarded – 6 out of 6

Question Two (Higher Tier)

The table below shows the changes that have taken place in employment in the three sectors of the economy in the County of Wetland during the period 1960 to 2000.

Year	Primary Sector	Secondary Sector	Tertiary Sector
1960	10,000	120,000	180,000
1980	7000	90,000	230,000
2000	5000	70,000	260,000

a) Explain how the importance of the secondary sector in Wetland may have changed in the period 1960 to 2000. **(4)**

b) To what extent are the changes in employment likely to have caused problems for the population of Wetland? Give reasons for your answer. **(8)**

Student Answer

a) Secondary production may be more important because more goods may be being produced in 2000 than in 1960 even though employment has fallen. If output has gone up this will be good for other businesses, both secondary and tertiary, which supply goods and services.

b) The changes in population are likely to cause problems because there will be a lot of people unemployed in the primary and secondary sector. There will also be less money given out in these sectors so the people who work in them will have less money to spend. The changes will also be good because there will be more jobs available in the tertiary sector therefore there will be more money to spend. There will also be more services provided for the people.

Chris

What the Examiner Says

a) The answer here is short – and sweet. Chris has been able to see beyond the fall in employment to suggest that production may not have fallen also. He has also been able to suggest how its production links with the tertiary sector.

Marks awarded – 4 out of 4

b) Chris's approach here is good – he might well have remembered the idea of 'writing frames' because he writes about both problems and advantages and this means that the answer reaches Level 2. The answer is spoilt, though, by a lack of detail and precision and development. For example, from the figures it can be shown that there is more employment in 2000 than in 1980 or in 1960. However, whilst some workers previously employed in the primary and secondary sectors will have been able to find jobs in the expanded tertiary sector, others may not – perhaps because they were too old or incapable of retraining to develop the new skills that they would need. It would also be necessary to know whether their new jobs in the tertiary sector were full or part-time and whether they were lower or higher paid than the jobs they left in the primary and secondary sectors.

This is a Level 2 (5–8) – Marks awarded – 5 out of 8

Question Three (a) Common Question b) Higher Tier

Millbank Farm in Wetland produces wheat. Abbey Mills Ltd use wheat to produce flour. Scanlons is a small bakery. Mr Scanlon makes fresh bread daily and sells it to the public in his shop.

a) State which sector of the economy each business is in. **(3)**
b) Explain fully how these businesses are interdependent. **(6)**

Student Answer

a) Millbank Farm, which produces wheat, is in the primary sector, Abbey Mills is in the secondary sector and Scanlons is in the tertiary sector.

b) These businesses are interdependent because Abbey Mills Ltd who are in the secondary sector depend on Millbank Farm who are in the primary sector to produce wheat so that they can produce flour. They need to produce the flour so that Scanlons, which is a small bakery in the tertiary sector, can make the fresh bread every day to sell to the public.

Danny

What the Examiner Says

a) Danny gets full marks for correctly identifying the sector that each business operates in.

Marks awarded – 3 out of 3

b) The answer tells only half the story! Danny explains how the secondary sector depends on the primary sector and the tertiary sector depends on the secondary. However, the dependency goes both ways. Millbank Farm, as a primary producer, depends on the success of Abbey Mills, the secondary producer, for its market, as Abbey Mills depends on the tertiary producer, Scanlons. To push the line of argument even further, it could be explained that the tertiary sector depends on the primary sector and vice versa

Level One (1–3) – Marks awarded – 3 out of 6

Question Four (Common Question)

State, giving your reasons, **two** objectives that may be suitable for each of the following:

a) Caroline's Cakes   This is a new shop. Caroline wants to set objectives for the first year that she is in business.
b) Wetland County Council.
c) Dearden Pottery Ltd   Dearden Pottery Ltd has been in business for five years. It has established itself in the pottery business in the UK. **(3 × 4 = 12)**

Student Answer

a) Caroline's shop is so new one of her main objectives for the first year should be survival. Many new businesses fail within just a few months of opening and so surviving the first year would be seen as an achievement. The other important objective would be to make a profit. All businesses need to make a profit in order to be successful, survive and grow. However, Caroline needs to be careful that she does not try to maximise her profits as customers may feel that they are not being treated well and sales could fall.

b) Wetland County Council's main objective should be to provide a service because their job is to serve the local community. The only other objective that a council may consider would be to make a profit in order to improve facilities by holding fund raising events.

c) Dearden Pottery Ltd has already established itself in the pottery business and has been in business for five years. However they may still see sales growth as an important objective. This does not necessarily mean making more profit, but they could open more shops in different areas, this way the business will grow.

Kathryn

What the Examiner Says

a) Kathryn correctly identifies the importance of survival for new businesses and provides useful information to emphasise how difficult this is. She also correctly identifies that the business may aim to make a profit and that this would allow further growth in the future. The point about profit maximisation is a good one – though it could have been expressed more clearly. Kathryn could also have developed the point about survival further by, for example, explaining the need to build up regular custom and ensuring that she produces a range of goods that is in demand. However, she did not need to do this – remember, there will usually be several possible answers to get the full marks!

Marks awarded – 4 out of 4

b) Kathryn scores marks for suggesting that the provision of a quality service is an appropriate objective for Wetland County Council and for identifying that it exists to serve the local community. The answer otherwise lacks some clarity. Kathryn needed to explain that as a Council, Wetland does not exist to make a profit. Also, a Council would be unlikely to raise money through fund-raising events – the objective might be to raise revenue in order to finance more or better services. If so, the Council would be likely to raise the money by increasing the Council Tax or seeking grants from central government or, possibly, the European Union.

Marks awarded – 2 out of 4

c) Kathryn makes some relevant points here – the business has become established, it should consider growth. Again, there is some lack of clarity. It is likely that the objective in terms of sales might be expressed in terms of a percentage rate of growth, a target figure in revenue terms or a certain percentage share of the overall market. She might also have explained what she meant by different areas – different regions in the UK and/or exporting abroad. Providing good quality pottery/service is also an appropriate objective and Kathryn might have developed this point further – does this need a change to the firm's marketing strategy? Certainly, providing a quality product and service will help to maintain customer confidence in the business.

Marks awarded – 2 out of 4

Question Five (Higher Tier)

Redborough Council is planning to build a new industrial estate on the edge of the town.

State and explain how stakeholders in the development may be affected if it goes ahead.

(10)

Student Answer

Some stakeholders will be pleased by the development whilst others will not. Those that will be pleased will be:

- *The businesses that will locate on the industrial estate because they will have brand new factories.*
- *Workers who get jobs in the new factories.*
- *Other businesses in the local community will be pleased because they may provide the new businesses with raw materials or with services. For example, a sandwich bar may be able to increase its sales by providing a delivery service to the workers on the new estate. Other local business may also get more sales because the people who work on the new estate may have more income and more money to spend which they spend in local shops and businesses.*
- *The Council, because the businesses will have to pay taxes to the Council.*

The people who will not be pleased will be:

- *The people who live near the new industrial estate – it may be an eyesore, it will mean more traffic in their area of town leading to congestion and noise and air pollution.*
- *Environmental groups may object if the estate is built on agricultural land which makes the area more built up. It is also possible that the land that is built on is the natural habitat for wildlife or for a certain kind of plant.*
- *Some competitors may not be pleased – the new firms may be able to produce at a lower cost because they are in new, modern factories. This may make it difficult for the older firms to compete.*

Ismat

What the Examiner Says

Ismat has produced a very good and very neatly written answer. It identifies both the benefits and the costs of the development – she may have used the writing frame suggested in the Introduction to the book to revise and to plan the work. Not only does she provide a comprehensive list of possible benefits and problems, she develops each point clearly and fully and gives appropriate examples.

Marks awarded – 10 out of 10

Types of Business Organisation

SECTION 2

Revision Material

KNOWLEDGE HIERARCHY: LIST OF THINGS TO KNOW ABOUT TYPES OF BUSINESS ORGANSIATION

This information is intended to provide a quick reminder. Your notes, and the information in the textbook you have used, should provide more detailed information and examples.

Topic	Key Features	Detail	Further Information
Sole Trader e.g. local window cleaner, plumber, etc.	• Unlimited Liability	• Owner's possessions at risk if declared bankrupt	• Bankrupt = debts greater than assets
	• Unincorporated	• Owner and business same legal person	
• The business is owned by one person	• Usually small in size	• Large number of this type of business	• Many self-employed people are sole traders
	• Income Tax paid on profits		
• The business may employ one person (the owner) or a number of people	• Advantages	• Easy to set up • Owner keeps all the profits	• No cost involved
	• Disadvantages	• Owner makes all the decisions	

Topic	Key Features	Detail	Further Information
Sole Trader *cont.*		• May not have enough capital for expansion • No continuity if owner dies • May have a skill shortage	• Disadvantages can be overcome by becoming another type of business organisation

Topic	Key Features	Detail	Further Information
Partnership e.g. most doctors, dentists and solicitors	• Unlimited Liability	• Owners' possessions at risk if declared bankrupt	• Bankrupt = debts greater than assets
	• Unincorporated	• Owners and business same legal person(s)	
• Minimum of 2 and maximum of 20 partners	• Usually have a Deed of Partnership	• Legal agreement detailing who is responsible for what	
	• Income Tax paid on profits		
	• Advantages	• Possibility of Sleeping Partners • Easy to set up • More owners	• Provide capital, not management • Divide management responsibilities • Possibility of more capital available
	• Disadvantages	• Profits (and Losses) must be shared • Possibility of disagreements	• Deed of Partnership may state how these are to be shared

Topic	Key Feature	Detail	Further Explanation
Private Limited Company (Ltd) e.g. Sainsburys Supermarket Ltd, Derby County Football Club Ltd	• Limited Liability • Incorporated	• Private possessions not at risk in the event of liquidation • Business is separate legal body from shareholders	• Liquidation = paying off debts by selling assets

Topic	Key Feature	Detail	Further Explanation
Private Limited Company (Ltd) *cont.*	• Owned by shareholders	• Board of Directors elected by shareholders • Profit paid to shareholders as dividend	• Election takes place at AGM • Some profit may be retained
	• Corporation Tax paid on profits		
	• Advantage	• Can raise capital through sales of shares	
	• Disadvantages	• Limited finance available through share sale • Some financial information has to be made public	• Cannot sell shares to raise finance via the Stock Market

Topic	Key Feature	Detail	Further Explanation
Public Limited Company (plc) e.g. Marks and Spencer plc, Tesco plc	• Limited Liability	• Private possessions not at risk in the event of liquidation	• Liquidation = paying off debts by selling assets
	• Incorporated	• Business is separate legal body from shareholders	
	• Usually a very large company		
	• Corporation Tax paid on profits		
	• Must have issued share capital in excess of £50 000		
	• Advantage	• Can raise large amounts of finance	• Share can be offered for sale to the general public as a means of raising finance
	• Disadvantages	• Business can be taken over if sufficient shares are obtained • No privacy	• Financial information has to be available for public inspection

Topic	Key Feature	Detail	Further Explanation
Other Types of Business Organisation	• **Franchise** e.g. Benetton, McDonalds, Body Shop	• Can trade as any of the four types of business organisation • Franchises are a type of marketing arrangement	• Franchisee provides advertising, advice, a tried and tested product • Franchise is often a well-known name • Franchisee pays a Royalty in return and can be expensive to set up
	• **Multinational** e.g. Ford Motor Company, Unilever, Nokia	• Usually very large businesses	• Multinational companies located in more than one country • Located near to market • Often lower manufacturing costs in other countries • Save on high transport costs to distant markets • Economies of large scale production may be lost by having several manufacturing facilities
	• **Holding Company** e.g. Dixons Group plc, Centrica plc	• Own other businesses • Usually large	• May gain economies of scale • May trade under different names or brand names • Larger market can be targeted • Easier to establish new businesses as markets change
	• **Co-operative** Producer/ Manufacturer	• Co-operatives popular for agricultural businesses where machinery can be shared	• Costs can be shared

Topic	Key Feature	Detail	Further Explanation
Other Types of Business Organisation *cont*	• **Co-operative** *cont*	• Some manufacturing businesses operate as worker co-operatives • Workers are also the owners of the business • Often set up by workers to protect jobs when a business is faced with closure	• Workers make the decisions

PUTTING IT IN CONTEXT

Sole trader businesses are suitable for small-scale operations where the capital needed can be provided out of the owner's (and probably his or her family's) savings, supplemented perhaps by a loan from a bank. Graham Thompson started a plumbing business as a sole trader. After four successful years, during which he developed a reputation locally for providing a high quality service, Graham wanted to expand the business so that it provided a wider range of services for business and domestic customers.

Graham needed to move to larger premises, to employ electricians and decorators and provide additional vehicles for these workers to use.

Graham took on a *partner*, partly to provide some of the additional capital needed but also to give him help in managing the business. The new partner, Ashley Hanson, had been an office manager. Ashley now ran the administration side of the business. When the partnership was formed, Graham drew up a *Deed of Partnership* clarifying how much capital each partner had provided and how any profit would be distributed, as well as stating the responsibilities of each partner. He knew it would help prevent possible conflict in the future.

Graham's sister, Maria, had also gone into business. With her husband, she had applied to run a Body Shop *franchise*. They decided that, in the light of their limited business experience, the advice they would receive, the marketing expertise and the tried and tested product range the franchiser would provide, it would be worth the loss of control and the expensive royalty charge they would have to pay. Maria and her husband had also decided that, with set-up costs of £350,000 financed by their own savings, a mortgage, bank loan and generous trade credit terms from the franchiser to purchase stock, they needed *limited liability* status. They decided that trading as a *private limited company* was the only alternative as the business was not large enough to make it worthwhile becoming a *public limited company*. Their business would not need the large injection of funds that public limited companies are able to obtain by selling to large numbers of shareholders. Being a private limited company meant that they did not need to make shares available through the Stock Exchange and so, as the two main shareholders, Maria and her husband would be able to maintain control. They knew that people would have access to their accounts if they wanted it.

One of the first things that Maria did when setting up the business was to draw up an *organisation chart* showing who is responsible for what. Whilst the business did not employ many workers, it allowed Maria to double check that she had people in place to do all the different jobs that were necessary. She also knew that the managers would be clear about for whom they were responsible and the workers clear about to whom they were responsible. Although the business was organised as a hierarchy, with her as the Managing Director, it was not a very tall organisation and this meant that communication between people in the different layers was not too complicated.

 ## ACTIVITIES

ACTIVITY ONE
Devise a *mind map* showing the advantages and disadvantages of operating a business as a Sole Trader.

ACTIVITY TWO
a) Draw an organisation chart for any one of the following: your School; a business you have studied; a business for which you have worked. The starting point may be the person in charge or the owner of the business.
   - How many different departments or sections does your organisation have?
   - What are the names of the staff?
   - Do you know their job titles?
   - Who are their line managers?
   - What type of business organisation is it?
b) How and why might the organisation chart need to change as the business changes?

ACTIVITY THREE
List some possible reasons for and against a business considering changing from a:

- Sole Trader to a Partnership
- Partnership to a Private Limited Company
- Private Limited Company to a Public Limited Company

ACTIVITY FOUR
The table below gives clues to some of the terms used when considering the key features of different types of business organisation. See if you can work out the answer to each clue.

Clue	Term
Helps protect your personal possessions if your business becomes insolvent.	
Usually paid to Shareholders twice a year – if you are lucky!	
Type of business where the owner keeps all the profits.	
There can be a maximum of 20 of these.	
This type of business is usually found in several countries.	
Usually elected by Shareholders at the Annual General Meeting	
If over £50,000 of shares have been issued, the business is probably one of these.	
This type of business can't sell them to the General Public in order to raise finance.	
The name of the payment made to the franchiser for the right to use a business name.	
A part owner of a business who invests money in it but takes no part in its day-to-day running.	
This type of business allows other businesses it owns to operate under different names.	
Two forms of business have to make these available for public inspection.	

QUESTION TYPES TO EXPECT

AQA 'A' questions may ask you to give the meaning and examples of terms such as:

- *Limited and Unlimited Liability*
- *Insolvency and Bankruptcy*
- *Ltd and PLC*
- *Incorporated and Unincorporated*
- *Board of Directors*
- *Shareholders*
- *Franchise, Franchisee, Franchiser, Royalty*
- *Multinational or Holding Company*

and many other business terms.

Other questions for both AQA 'A' and 'B' may ask you to:

- *give or explain a certain number of advantages or disadvantages of one or two of the different types of business organisation.*
- *give or explain a number of key features about a particular form of business organisation.*

More difficult questions, which are likely to require a detailed response, may ask you to:

- advise or evaluate the appropriateness of a particular form of business organisation, based on some information which has been provided.
- recommend, giving reasons, appropriate ways for a given type of business to obtain additional finance.
- consider whether it would be better to operate as one type of business or another.

Some examples of these types of questions and student answers are given in the following section. Look carefully at what the question is asking you to do; how the student has answered the question; what the examiner thinks of the answer.

TYPES OF BUSINESS ORGANISATION: SPECIMEN QUESTIONS

Question One (Higher Tier)

James Brown has recently inherited some money which he wants to invest by setting up his own business. He has decided that a vacant shop unit near to where he lives would be ideal for a fast food restaurant and, given that he has worked for Pizza Supreme for four years as a restaurant manager, he will start a take-away pizza business. However, he cannot decide whether to set up as an independent business or become part of a well-known pizza franchise.

Discuss the advantages and disadvantages of each option. Giving reasons, say which one you would recommend James to do. **(12)**

Student Answer

If James were to set up as an independent business, money would need to be spent on employing staff, promoting the business, as well as purchasing a shop unit. This means a considerable amount of initial outlay would be needed and also a considerable amount of risk would be involved.

If James were to buy a well-known pizza franchise, the initial outlay on a unit for the shop equipment would not be needed. The company would already be established and therefore there would be no need for promotion. The main problem with a franchise is that there would be less flexibility.

If, for example, a franchise of Domino Pizza is purchased, the same standards are usually required. This means product ranges must be the same and if demand for a certain product is higher then promotions must be franchise-wide.

If James purchased a shop unit and set up as a sole trader he has far fewer limitations to his business operation. After he established himself with a name and certain style of pizza he would be able to be far more profitable.

Matthew

Question Two (Common Question)

Large companies can sometimes experience problems which are not a problem to smaller companies. Shown below are two possible problems:

- communication difficulties
- increased costs of production

Explain, giving examples, how these problems may affect a company. Give reasons for your answers.   **(12)**

Student Answer

Large companies experience problems which are not a problem to smaller companies because of their different hierarchical structures. The different types of hierarchy can cause communication problems. Smaller companies tend not to have communication problems because there are fewer people working there. Also with larger companies, there are different departments such as marketing, human resources, finance, etc. These departments may not communicate which may cause problems overall. However, through simple communication such as meetings and email these problems may be overcome.

For a large company to have increased costs of production it would mean increased costs for the customer. Customers may then start shopping at smaller companies where it is likely that they may then start to expand. By expanding they are creating more competition for the larger companies which will want to keep their share of the market. Also this may stop the company from achieving economies of scale. This may not allow the business to expand. Increased costs of production can also lead to a loss of jobs. This may cause the company to downsize.

Charlotte

What the Examiner Says

Charlotte has, quite correctly, attempted to organise the answer into two separate parts, making it easier for the examiner to mark. This is important, as a clearly set out answer is an important requirement for the exam.

Unfortunately, both parts of the answer are very confused and fall well short of actually answering the question which has been set. In the first part, there is clearly some understanding that larger organisations will have more of a hierarchical structure but there is no mention of the length of the Chain of Command or the width of the Span of Control. Both of these can contribute to communication problems in terms of the time it may take for information to be passed on or the clarity of the information received by the end user. There is though, recognition that smaller businesses with fewer employees usually have fewer communication problems because of the relative ease with which information can be passed on. Charlotte could have mentioned more than just email and meetings as methods which might go some way to improving communication. Examples of why and how these methods might help could have been given.

In the second part of the answer there is a great deal of confusion. Terms such as economies of scale are used but without showing any real understanding of what the term means and how this type of information could have been used to answer the question. Charlotte has correctly identified that increased costs do affect the selling price of a product or service which has to be paid by the consumer. As a result of this, consumers may choose to go elsewhere. There is no mention of the way in which businesses attempt to control costs nor is there any mention of the different types of costs involved.

This candidate has probably done sufficient to earn a Level 2 (5–8 marks) mark – but only just. There is some understanding but there are too many inaccurate and poorly explained points. A mark of only 5 out of 12 is likely to have been awarded.

Question Three (Common Question)

Speedy Block, a partnership specialising in block paving for patios and drives, has been in business for just over two years. It has been trading very successfully and the two brothers who run the business are considering converting the company to a private limited company.

a) Explain, giving reasons, which type of business organisation you would recommend for Speedy Block. **(8)**

b) Speedy Block has become a successful business in a short time. Not all new businesses are successful. Discuss the factors which might cause a new business to fail. **(8)**

Student Answer

a) There are pros and cons of becoming an incorporated business. If the business remains a partnership, it will face unlimited liability. This is a considerable risk despite the recent success of the business. Being unincorporated also means having to make all decisions facing the business. Security, then, is the principle reason for becoming incorporated. Such a move would enable the business to have limited liability. Conversely, it is not possible to use shares as a means of raising funds; private limited company shares may not be advertised for sale outside the business if the business were to decide on this form of organisation. I would not recommend the business attempt conversion to a public limited company as the business would have to sell over £50,000 worth of shares before it could start trading.

b) Not all businesses are successful. There are many factors which can affect the success of a business, particularly a new one. Such things as the degree of competition in the market in which the business is trading; the amount of work or orders it receives; the way in which the business controls its costs; the price it charges in relation to the costs of doing something will all have an effect on the success of the business. New businesses have particular problems. One of the most significant will be establishing itself in the market place and getting its name known. Without this it is unlikely to get sufficient work. Many new businesses are also set up through loans. These debts have to be repaid with interest and these businesses have to be particularly hard working and profitable if they are to generate sufficient finance to meet the repayments. Establishing a reputation will also be important for a new business and this can be difficult to do until work has been completed for customers.

Louise

What the Examiner Says

a) Louise has correctly identified one of the key problems facing businesses when deciding on the type of business organisation – limited or unlimited liability. However, no detail has been given as to the advantages and disadvantages of this key feature other than to make some reference to security. This particular point should have been developed and explained fully in terms of the effects on the personal possessions of the owner(s) of a business in the event of bankruptcy/liquidation.

There are, of course, other issues relating to the type of business organisation to choose and these should have been discussed more fully. However, Louise does have some understanding of the types of business organisation available but should have given the advantages and disadvantages of each type of business organisation referred to in the question. This would have helped when making a recommendation – as required by the question. The question did not require any reference to be made to Public Limited Companies but it did require some consideration of the relevance of remaining in business as a Partnership.

Marks awarded – 4 out of 8

b) This is a good, detailed answer, which considers a large number of factors which are likely to have an effect on the success of a business. The candidate has also attempted to relate these factors to the problems which new businesses, in particular, are likely to face.

Marks awarded – 7 out of 8

Question Four (Higher Tier)

Shown below is some information for HOP IT plc, an extremely successful low cost airline. Using this information, and any other you have available, answer the questions which follow.

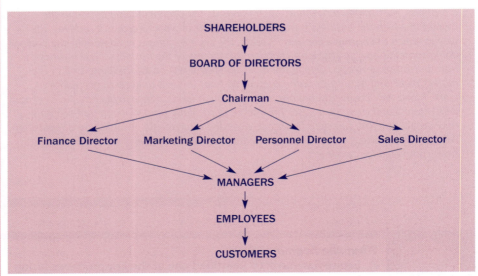

a) Explain why Public Limited Companies, such as HOP IT plc, have a Board of Directors. **(6)**

b) Suggest and explain ONE problem to HOP IT plc of trading as a Public Limited Company. **(4)**

c) Explain why shareholders might have invested money into a company such as HOP IT plc. **(4)**

d) Name TWO groups of Stakeholders in HOP IT plc and suggest why they have an interest in the company. **(8)**

Student Answer

a) *Because a Public Limited company has limited liability and so if the business gets into financial difficulties, it would be the Board of Directors that would lose their house, etc. to pay off the debts. This is instead of the chairman or shareholders.*

b) *Public Limited Companies can't advertise their shares on the stock market. This reduces the number of possible investors for the company and makes it difficult for them to generate money.*

c) *They are a low cost airline so customers will like using them to travel. Therefore, income will increase and the higher the income and lower the output, the greater the profit. Dividends may therefore increase.*

d) *Passengers – they want a quick comfortable journey for a low price and a low risk factor.*

   Staff – they are looking to give passengers a good service so their chances of promotion are increased. They want loyal customers so sales revenue and net profit will increase. Therefore chance of pay rises are greater.

   Nisha

What the Examiner Says

a) Nisha has not answered the question and clearly does not have any understanding of limited liability. Limited Liability is irrelevant in terms of answering the question. No mention has been made about how the Board of Directors is elected by shareholders to make important decisions about the direction that the business will take and to oversee, on behalf of shareholders, the operation of the business.

Marks awarded – 0 out of 6

b) Whilst Nisha correctly identifies that shares are sold as a means of raising finance she has incorrectly stated that **Public** Limited Companies are unable to do this. Perhaps a more appropriate answer might have been to identify the problems regarding the possibility of a take-over if one person or organisation obtains a large number of shares. Secondly, she could have mentioned the fact that a plc needs to make financial information available to the general public which may be of advantage to competitors.

Marks awarded – 2 out of 4

c) Nisha has correctly identified that the demand for low cost air travel is increasing leading to an increase in income for the business. Nisha has also correctly identified that this may lead to an increase in profits leading to larger dividends for shareholders. However, there is some confusion with regard to output and costs.

Marks awarded – 3 out of 4

49

d) Two groups of stakeholders have been correctly identified. The explanation for passengers, although brief, is appropriate. As regards staff, a more detailed response has been provided which is basically correct although not as clearly expressed/explained as it could have been.

Marks awarded – 5 out of 8

Question Five (Common Question)

The figure shows the structure for a branch of Carvers, a national chain of electrical retailers. There are five levels in the hierarchy.

a) Discuss whether it would be a good idea for Carvers to display this organisational structure in each of their branches. **(6 marks)**

b) Discuss whether it would be a good idea for Carvers to remove one level of the hierarchy, for instance, the junior managers. **(8 marks)**

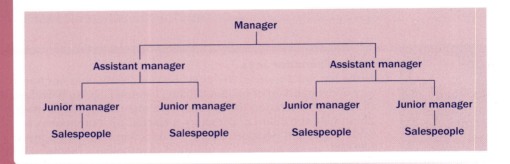

Student Answer

(a)   If Carvers put their organisation chart on display, this would let both the customers and the employees know about the structure. This would show that they are an open company, willing to share information. However, there is no real need for the business to share this information with customers, as they do not need to know this information.

The employees (like the salespeople and junior managers) would know who their line managers were and the route for promotion for them would be made clear. However, this would only need to be on display for the employees, say in their coffee making area. On the other hand, displaying the structure could actually have a bad effect as it would let the customers know who the most junior people working there were and could lead them to overlooking them and going to find a manager instead. This could demotivate the junior staff. Because of this, I do not think that it would be a good idea for Carvers to display the structure.

b) *If Carvers removed a layer of the chart this would give more responsibility to those further down the organisation. If there were fewer tiers, this would mean communication between the top and bottom of the organisation would be better. It would also make it easier for salespeople to be promoted to managerial positions and this would motivate them to do better. On the downside, it could mean a greater workload for the assistant managers and they would probably want to be paid more money for this.*

Jenny

What the Examiner Says

a) Jenny has given a good answer to the question. She has reached the top level by making a clear judgement based on her discussion of the question. To do this she has weighed up firstly, who would actually see the organisation chart and secondly, what use they would make of it. She rightly points out that the chart would be of little interest to Carvers' customers (although does not expand on why this is the case) but that it could actually have a negative effect if they were to see that there are more senior people that they could turn to for help. Finally, Jenny makes a decision which is justified by the discussion.

There is clear analysis of the question and clear judgement, although the analysis could have been more detailed.

Marks awarded 5 out of 6

b) Although Jenny uses good technique with this answer (using devices like 'on the one hand' and 'on the downside' to show that a comparison is being made) she does not actually answer the question. Would it be a good idea or not? This means that she can not gain the marks for making a judgement. This is a good analysis but only gets half the marks available because a judgement has not been made.

Marks awarded 4 out of 8

Question Six (Common Question)

Bill Jones, a Sole Trader, has been running a small but successful electronic circuit board manufacturing business for several years. At the moment he has five employees.

His accountant has advised him to consider converting to a Limited Liability form of business organisation. He does not know what to do and has asked for your help.

Advise Bill of the advantages and disadvantages of staying as a Sole Trader or converting to a Limited Liability business. **(12)**

Student Answer

As a Sole Trader and owner of a small business there are a number of advantages. He has sole ownership of the business and therefore full control of the way in which it is run. He can decide the hours of work, shift patterns and wage rates for workers, etc. If he converted to a limited company, unless he kept all the shares in the business, he may lose control to other shareholders.

There are a number of drawbacks to operating as a Sole Trader. There may be no one to cover his position should he fall ill. He holds full responsibility for the running of the business and should it get into trouble financially any debts may have to be paid by Bill even if this means having to sell his personal possessions. With limited liability, this element of risk is removed and he would only stand to lose his initial investment if the business were to get into financial trouble.

Although there is more risk running as a Sole Trader, it would be better for this small business to stay unchanged. The business is successful and in the technology market, which has a high level of investment and is continuously expanding, the risk of running into trouble is minimal. Currently it might be better for Mr Jones to stay in full control and he should only consider converting to limited liability if the business expands significantly and/or takes on more risk.

Katie

What the Examiner Says

Katie has offered a lot of sound advice, as required by the question. A recommendation, backed up by reasons, has also been made. The answer, perhaps, dwells a little too much on the aspect of limited versus unlimited liability. Some consideration might have been given to the problems which many small businesses face when seeking to raise additional finance. However, Katie has recognised the key advantages/disadvantages of the Sole Trader form of business organisation. Some mention should also have been made about some of the problems that exist in becoming a Limited Company. For instance, the need to make some financial information available to the public which may be of use to competitors.

This is a good answer and is clearly worth Level 3 (9–12 marks)

Marks awarded – 10 out of 12

Accounting and Finance

SECTION 3

Money is the lifeblood of a business. Too little, and the business is in danger of stopping. Too much, and the business may not use it as effectively as it should. As a result, most businesses spend a lot of time managing money, making sure that there is enough of it at the right time. Much of this work is done by accountants who prepare detailed financial statements which help the managers of the business to make decisions.

Whilst not all businesses need be profit-making, most of them are. Knowing whether the business is operating at a profit or a loss is very important. However, some businesses fail, not because they are unprofitable, but because they simply run out of money. Customers may not have paid for their goods; too much money may be tied up in stock; bills are more than anticipated or not enough has been sold. On the other hand, a business will fail if it cannot sell its products or services at a profit.

Revision Material

KNOWLEDGE HIERARCHY: LIST OF THINGS TO KNOW ABOUT TYPES OF BUSINESS ORGANSIATION

This information is intended to provide a quick reminder. Your notes, and the information in the textbook you have used, should provide more detailed information and examples.

Topic	Key Features	Detail	Further Information
Sources of finance e.g. Share Issue; Owners funds Bank loans	• Large number of different sources	• Type of finance used depends on a range of factors • The amount required, the length of time and the cost are all important considerations	• Factors include the type of business wishing to use the finance; the use to which the finance will be put

Topic	Key Features	Detail	Further Information
Sources of finance *cont.*	• Two basic types of finance – Internal and External	• Internal finance comes from within the business	• Several different types, e.g. Retained Profit; selling assets for cash; owners funds
		• Advantages	• Money does not have to be paid back • No interest to be paid
		• Disadvantage	• Opportunity cost involved
		• External finance is provided from outside the business	• Many different types, e.g. loan; mortgage
		• Advantage	• Successful businesses find it easier to obtain this type of finance
		• Disadvantages	• Usually a cost involved • A form of security often needed
	• Combination of different sources of finance often used	• Helps overcome or reduce some of the disadvantages	

Topic	Key Features	Detail	Further Information
Profit When Total Revenue from sales is greater then Total Cost	• Key objective of most businesses • Not all businesses are profit-making	• Examples of non-profit making businesses are charities	
	• Several different types of profit	• Gross Profit, Net Profit, Operating Profit are all calculated by business	
	• Size of the profit made can be used to judge success	• Profit comparisons can be made with previous years • Profit performance can be compared to other (similar) businesses	• Ratio analysis used to compare performance • Gross Profit to Sales and Net Profit to Sales ratios used to compare performance

Topic	Key Features	Detail	Further Information
Profit *cont.*			• Profit Margin or Mark-up are also used by businesses
	• Large number of factors which can influence the size of the profit made	• Fierce competition may reduce sales, prices and therefore profit • Poor cost control may reduce profit	
	• Profit is often re-invested in the business	• Retained profit is used to help fund the activities of the business • Some profit paid to shareholders	• Dividends are a payment made to shareholders from profits not retained by the business
	• Loss-making businesses rarely survive for long		
	• New businesses often find it hard to make a profit in the first few years of trading	• New businesses have high start-up costs	• New businesses usually need to buy a lot of equipment

Topic	Key Features	Detail	Further Information
Cash Flow Needs to be managed to ensure the business does not run out of cash	• The flow of money in and out of a business	• Businesses attempt to forecast the flow of money in and out of the business	• A forecast covers a particular time period – usually a month • Forecasted income minus forecasted expenditure shows how much money the business might have available
		• Some businesses with seasonal activities may have a difficult cash flow to manage	• Ice cream sellers and fireworks manufacturers have sales which fall at particular times • Supermarkets tend to have a fairly even flow of cash as people need food all the year round

Topic	Key Features	Detail	Further Information
Cash Flow *cont*	• Cash Flow is not a profit calculation	• Surplus cash represents a positive cash balance • A negative cash balance may mean the business has to take action	• A business needs to use its cash surplus effectively • Delaying payment, selling more or chasing up debts may help the cash position • Borrowing; cutting costs; selling more goods may help the business overcome a temporary negative cash balance

Topic	Key Features	Detail	Further Information
The final Accounts of a Business Two main documents – the Trading, Profit and Loss Account; The Balance Sheet. Documents are completed quarterly, half-yearly or yearly	• Trading Profit and Loss Account used to calculate profit or loss • Balance Sheet states what the business owns and owes	• Accounts are read by a large number of interested stakeholders • Assets of a business must always equal the Liabilities • Information in the documents can be used to compare performance by using Ratio analysis	• Trading Profit and Loss Account shows the different types of profit and what has happened to it • Balance Sheet lists all the Assets and Liabilities of the business • Balance Sheet also shows where the business has got its money from and how it has been used • Assets and Liabilities are listed according to liquidity
	• Accounting information details exactly what has happened to the business over a period of time	• Recognising the trend over time is important • Comparisons can be made with other businesses • Each Ratio has an 'ideal' answer	• Current Ratio ideal answer is around 2 • Acid Test ideal answer is between 0.8 and 1

Topic	Key Features	Detail	Further Information
The final Accounts of a Business *cont*			• Both ratios measure the liquidity of the business
	• Ratios used to compare if the business is getting better or worse over time	• Results either side of the ideal answer indicate that the business is not managing its resources effectively	
		• Working Capital is another test of how much money the business has available for its day-to-day needs	• A negative Working Capital figure indicates that the business is in danger of running out of cash for day-to-day activities
		• Return on Capital Employed (ROCE) is yet another financial measure	• ROCE compares the relationship between the profit made and the amount of money (capital) needed to generate it

PUTTING IT IN CONTEXT

Sam Brown's garden services business – Garden Designs Ltd – is a real success story. Sam started the business as a sole trader just over five years ago. It had very little equipment and only enough work to employ Sam. It is now a very successful and profitable private limited company employing four full-time and several part-time workers. One of the best decisions she made when she started the business was to take her friend's advise to use the services of an accountant. The accountant would be able to prepare her financial statements and offer business advice.

As the business grew in size and needed more equipment, Sam's accountant was able to provide information about different *sources of finance* which might be available to help purchase the new equipment. Sam had not realised that only certain sources of finance were available to different types of business, nor had she realised the *costs* and *drawbacks* involved.

When she first started out in business, Sam had not realised how important it was for her to manage her *cash flow*. Some jobs, which she was given, needed large quantities of materials which had to be bought before starting. If the customer was a little slow in paying for the work Sam sometimes found that she was in danger of running out of money even though she knew that the prices she was charging more than covered the cost of the materials and her time. Sam quickly learned that getting *trade credit* from her suppliers, therefore delaying payment for goods, and making sure that customers paid promptly, helped to make sure that the business did not have cash-flow problems.

One of the most important jobs which Sam's accountant did for her business was to prepare her *final accounts.* Sam's *Trading, Profit and Loss Account* showed her exactly how much business she had done during the year and how much *profit* had been made. She could see clearly the *Sales Revenue* the business had earned and the *costs* involved in running the business. Her accountant explained, using a technique called *Ratio Analysis*, how to compare the information from one year with previous years so that Sam could see how much progress the businesses was making. Sam's *Balance Sheet* showed her *how much the business was worth* and *how much money was owed* by it. The Balance Sheet showed the value of all the *assets* and liabilities which the business had. Again, by comparing the information contained in the Balance Sheet with that from previous years it was possible to measure how financially secure her business was.

Sam now really understood why it was so important to pay such close attention to the finances of her business and what good advice her friend had given her.

ACTIVITIES

ACTIVITY ONE

The table below shows the main ratios used to compare financial performance. Complete the table by writing in the formula for each ratio and explain what the ratio tells you about the financial circumstances of the business.

Ratio	Formula	The purpose for which the ratio is used
Gross Profit to Sales		
Net Profit to Sales		
Acid Test		
Current Ratio		
Working Capital		
Return on Capital Employed (ROCE)		

ACTIVITIES *cont.*

ACTIVITY TWO

Work out the answers to the following questions which are based on the contents of a Trading Profit and Loss Account:

a) What does Sales Revenue minus Cost of Sales equal?
b) What is the amount of stock which a business has at the beginning of a trading period known as?
c) What is this amount of stock (referred to in Question b) known as at the end of the previous trading period?
d) What is subtracted from Gross Profit to calculate Net Profit?
e) What is the name given to the payment made from profits to the owners of a Limited Company?
f) What is money kept by the business, to pay for new equipment, known as?
g) All businesses have to pay tax on the profits which they make. What is the name given to the tax paid on profits by:
   i) Sole Traders and Partnerships?
   ii) Limited Companies?
h) Why might the Sales Revenue of a business change from one year to another?
i) Prepare a *Mind Map* showing the uses to which a Trading Profit and Loss Account is put by most businesses.

ACTIVITY THREE

Complete the following Balance Sheet by replacing **XXXXX** with the correct words or figures.

Balance Sheet for Garden Design Ltd as at 31 March 2003

	£	£	£
XXXXX Assets			
Plant and Equipment		25000	
Vehicles		30000	55000
XXXXX Assets			
Stock	5000		
Debtors	20000		
Bank	15000	40000	
Current XXXXX			
Overdraft	3000		
Trade Creditors	15000	XXXXX	
Net XXXXX Capital			XXXXX
NET XXXXX EMPLOYED			XXXXX
Shareholders Funds			
Ordinary Shares		30000	
Reserves and XXXXX Profit		45000	XXXXX
Long Term Liabilities			
Bank Loan		2000	2000
XXXXX EMPLOYED			77000

ACTIVITY FOUR

Using a grid outline similar to the one below:

a) List all the different sources of finance which you can think of.
b) Place a ✓ in the columns to the right of the source of finance to indicate whether that source is likely to be used by a particular type of business.
c) In the last column, suggest a use to which this source of finance may be put.

An example has been done for you.

Source of Finance	Sole Trader	Partnership	Private Limited Company	Public Limited Company	Example(s) of use of Finance
Sale of shares to the general public				✓	Capital is needed to finance an expansion programme or the purchase of another business

ACTIVITY FIVE

Make a copy of the following Cash Flow Outline.

	January £	February £	March £	April £	May £	June £
Opening Balance b/f						
INCOME:						
TOTAL INCOME						

	January £	February £	March £	April £	May £	June £
EXPENDITURE:						
TOTAL EXPENDITURE						
Closing Balance c/f						

a) Use the following information to draw up a Cash Flow Forecast for Garden Designs Ltd. The business starts off the time period with a balance of £1000. It expects sales in January to be £6000, rising by £2000 each month until April when sales peak and remain constant for the rest of the time period.

Expenditure is much more variable. Wages are expected to be constant for the first three months at £5000 and then increase to £6000 followed by two months at £7000. Insurance of £3000 is due in February and Accountancy Fees of £1000 are paid in April. Fuel costs are £100 per month except for May and June when the fuel bill is expected to double. Material costs are low in January at £1000 rising to £2000 in February. The monthly materials bill for the rest of the time period is expected to be £3000.

b) Explain possible reasons for the expected Cash Flow deficit in the early part of the year. Explain why the business may not be too concerned about the forecast deficit.

c) Explain why the business expects to have so much cash available at the end of the time period and why this may be important for this type of business.

d) Explain how businesses forecast their expected income and expenditure.

e) Complete an *Image Chain* detailing the sequence of events for the preparation and use of a Cash Flow Forecast such as the one you have just completed in a) above.

 # QUESTION TYPES TO EXPECT

AQA 'A' questions may ask you to give the meaning and examples of terms such as:

- *Fixed and Current Assets*
- *Current and Long Term Liabilities*
- *Gross, Net and Retained Profit*
- *Sales Revenue*

- *Cash Flow*
- *Internal and External Finance*
- *Different Sources of Finance*
- *Opportunity Cost*
- *Shareholders Funds and Dividends*

and many other business terms.

For both 'A' and 'B' specifications, using numerical data is an essential part of understanding accounting and finance. You should therefore expect to find a reasonable number of questions containing a numerical content. They are designed to test your ability to use, apply and evaluate numerical and financial data.

Numerical and financial data may be presented in a variety of ways. Pie charts, bar graphs, tables and financial documents are just some of the ways. Expect to find these ways in an examination question paper.

Examples of how numerical skills may be tested include:

- *calculating how much Sales Revenue, Profit, Expenditure or some other figure has changed from one year to another either as a simple figure, or as a percentage change.*
- *estimating how much additional finance the business may require to complete a project is another possibility.*
- *working out some of the missing figures from a Cash Flow Forecast; Trading, Profit and Loss Account; Balance Sheet.*
- *using Ratio Analysis to analyse the financial information of a business.*

Other questions, which may require detailed answers, might ask you to pass comment or provide some form of advice to the business. For instance:

- *Using the information available advise the business how it may overcome a particular problem.*
- *Evaluate the appropriateness of a particular course of action based on the information available.*
- *Recommend, giving reasons, alternative ways of financing the business.*

Some examples of these types of questions and student answers are given in the following section. Look carefully at what the question is asking you to do; how the student has answered the question; what the examiner thinks of the answer.

ACCOUNTING AND FINANCE: SPECIMEN QUESTIONS

Question One (Higher Tier)
The following table contains a summary of the information contained in the accounts of Bowton Engineering plc for the years ending 2001 and 2002. Read the information carefully and use it to help answer the questions which follow.

	2001	2002
Sales Revenue	£400m	£500m
Gross Profit	£80m	£120m
Net Profit	£20m	£25m
Dividend per Share	10p	11p

a) Discuss the factors which may have caused an increase in the Sales Revenue between 2001 and 2002. **(6)**

b) Comment on the performance of the business in 2002 compared to 2001. **(8)**

Student Answer

a)   An increase in sales revenue could be due to an increase in sales or a fall in costs which could be the result of economies of scale such as bulk buying. Or, an increase in selling price and a constant, or slight drop in sales, would result in an increased sales revenue.

b) Overall business performance in 2002 was much improved on that of 2001. As sales revenue has increased by £100m from £400m to £500m which led to an increased gross profit of £120m rather than £80m in 2001. This increased gross profit therefore led to an increase in the net profit by £5m from £20m to £25m which led to a higher dividend payment of 11p rather than 10p per share which had been paid previously. Therefore, Bowton Engineering had a much better year in 2002 than in 2001 which could have been due to many factors, e.g. an increase in sales; fall in production costs; increased selling price or an increased efficiency level.

Paul

What the Examiner Says

a) Whilst this may appear a brief answer, Paul has made a good attempt at answering the question. The reference to a fall in costs is irrelevant as costs would have no impact on the sales revenue earned by a business. Paul has recognised that even a slight drop in the number of items sold, with an increased selling price, could probably lead to an increase in the sales revenue. Making reference to elasticity could have extended this part of the answer. Some mention could have been made about the effect of competition on sales or the popularity of the product(s) being sold.

This is a Level 2 answer (4–6 marks)
Marks awarded – 4 out of 6

b) Paul's analysis of the financial information effectively restates the information in the table in text form. Some suggestions have been made to explain the differences in the figures between 2001 and 2002. What Paul has failed to do is to recognise that a ratio analysis comparison needs to be made between Gross Profit and Sales (24% compared to 20%) and Net Profit and Sales (5% compared with 5%) so that a more accurate comparison can be made between performances in 2002 compared with 2001. Had this been done, the conclusions drawn by Paul might have been different.

Other percentage comparisons could also have been made by calculating the percentage increase in Sales Revenue (25%) and comparing this with the percentage increase in both Gross Profit

(50%) and Net Profit (25%). Had this been done, comment could have been made on the increase in sales resulting in different percentage increases in the two measures of profit. Some form of explanation should have been offered as to why this was the case. For instance, costs of running the business have risen at the same rate as sales but costs of buying goods for re-sale have fallen, possibly because of economies of scale.

This is a Level 1 answer (1–3 marks)
Marks awarded – 3 out of 8

Question Two (Common Question)

The Board of Directors of Marby Plastics plc is considering investing in new computer-controlled manufacturing machinery. The Directors have considered the following methods of financing the new machinery.

Retained Profit   **Share Issue**   **Bank Loan**

Recommend to the Directors, giving reasons, which method of finance you would choose and which you would reject.   **(12)**

Student Answer

The Board of Directors of Marby Plastics has three options for financing the new machinery. The first option, Retained Profit, is only possible if the business has made a profit in previous years which it has not distributed to shareholders in the form of dividends. The main benefits of this source of finance is that no interest is payable as it is the company's own capital. A possible drawback of using this source of capital is that should the company need finance for any other purpose it will no longer be available. There is, therefore, an opportunity cost of using retained profit to fund the new equipment. Retained profit is an internal source of finance.

Share capital has the advantage of not needing to be paid back. However, selling shares may result in other people or organisations taking control of the business. Shareholders will also expect a return on their investment in the form of dividends. A bank loan, like share capital, is an external source of finance. A bank loan will have to repaid in full together with interest so this could possibly be an expensive source of finance if someone can be found who is prepared to lend the money.

In the light of this information, the best option for the company would probably be a combination of retained profit together with sale of a limited number of shares. This may help to overcome the disadvantages of each of these two options. A bank loan is probably the most costly of the three options.

Asif

What the Examiner Says

This is a very good answer. Asif has considered each option in turn and put forward some advantages and disadvantages. He has then gone on to make a recommendation, as required by the question. His solution is particularly interesting in that he has not put forward just one option but has suggested a combination. He has also given a justification for why he is recommending a combination. The only thing that he might have been able to add to his answer is that it can be costly to sell shares and there is no guarantee that sufficient shares will be purchased to finance the new investment.

This is a Level 3 (9 – 12 marks) answer
Marks awarded – 11 out of 12

Question Three (Common Question)

The following information is an extract from the Balance Sheets of Fiesta Manufacturing Ltd. Use the information to help answer some of the questions which follow.

	2000	2001	2002
CURRENT ASSETS	£m	£m	£m
Stock	440	980	1 400
Debtors	400	480	470
Cash at Bank and in hand	110	48	10
CURRENT LIABILITIES			
Creditors	210	360	560
Overdraft	300	520	640
ACID TEST RATIO	1	0.6	0.4

a) Explain the difference between Current Assets and Current Liabilities. **(3)**
b) Explain why sufficient working capital is important to a business like Fiesta Manufacturing Ltd. **(4)**
c) Comment on the changes in Fiesta Manufacturing Ltd's liquidity position. **(6)**
d) Recommend, to the business, how it might improve its liquidity. **(8)**

a)   The difference between current assets and current liabilities is that current assets are what the business owns and current liabilities are what the business owes.

b)   Working capital = Current Assets minus Current Liabilities. Working capital is the money required for the day-to-day running of the business. If the business does not have sufficient Working Capital it may not be able to pay workers or buy replacement stock.

c)   The Acid Test Ratio should preferably be between 0.8 and 1.0 in order for a business not to have liquidity problems. However, in 2001 and 2002 the Acid Test ratio dropped to a low figure. The business may therefore have a problem with its liquidity. The problem is due to a massive rise in creditors and overdraft, with only a small rise in debtors.

d)   This business appears to have a liquidity problem. There has been a significant increase in the value of stock between 2000 and 2002. Too much cash may be tied up in this asset and the business should look for ways of reducing stock levels. The business should also look into ways of encouraging debtors to pay up more quickly for goods received. Whilst the amount has not increased there is still a lot of money owed to Fiesta Manufacturing Ltd. If this were to happen, it may allow the business to reduce the size of its overdraft which has been increasing steadily.

Rachel

What the Examiner Says

a) Rachel's answer is correct. However, she perhaps should have provided a little bit more detail by stating that current liabilities can be turned into cash quickly and current liabilities have to be repaid usually with one year.

Marks awarded – 2 out of 3

b) This is a good answer. A definition of the term has been given together with an accurate explanation, with examples, of what the term means and how a lack of working capital may affect a business.

Marks awarded – 4 out of 4

c) The question has not been answered fully. Rachel has correctly identified that the Acid Test ratio is a measure of liquidity which has an ideal answer which the company has failed to achieve in 2001 and 2002. An attempt has been made to identify the reasons for the problem. However, she should have gone on to calculate the Current Ratio for each year so that an even more detailed comment on the firm's liquidity position could have been made. Had she done so, she would have seen that this ratio was also falling **and** below an acceptable level of safety.

Marks awarded – 4 out of 6

d) Although a relatively short answer, a good attempt has been made at answering this question. Good answers do not always have to be long-winded! The information in the question has been carefully analysed and sound solutions have been put forward which will have a significant impact on the liquidity of the business if carried out. Reference, perhaps, should have been made to the Current and Acid Test Ratios.

This is a Level 3 (7–8 marks) answer
Marks awarded – 7 out of 8

Question Four (Higher Tier)

Christine and John McCormack think they have a good business idea. However, before they can start their business they need a loan. Their local bank manager has said that he is not able to help until they provide a Cash Flow Forecast for their business idea. Unfortunately, they are not sure what to do and have asked you for help.

a) Explain to Christine and John, the contents and purpose of a Cash Flow Forecast. **(6)**
b) Giving examples, explain how the bank manager might use the information in the Cash Flow Forecast to decide whether to grant Christine and John the loan they have asked for. **(8)**

Student Answer

a) A cash flow forecast contains details of all the funds expected to flow into and out of the business in a certain period of time. This would include forecasts of sales income and the expenses which the business expects to have. This information then allows the business to work out when it may have a surplus or shortage of cash.

b) The bank manager will be able to use the information in the cash flow forecast to assess whether it is a good idea to lend the business money. Whilst the forecast does not calculate how much profit the business is likely to make it does show whether the business is likely to achieve sufficient sales income in relation to the costs of the running the business and whether the business is going to be able to afford to repay the loan. The forecast will help identify particular times when the business may be short of cash and when it may have a cash surplus. In addition to sales income, the forecast will also show other sources of income which Christine and John hope to have.

James

What the Examiner Says

a) A relatively brief answer. James could, and should, have provided a little more detail by giving examples of different types of expenses which most businesses usually have. No reference has been made to the fact that the amount of the cash surplus or deficit at the end of one month is carried forward to the beginning of the next month. Mention should also have been made of the fact that one of the purposes of the cash flow forecast is to help the business plan ahead and manage its cash efficiently, by looking to see if it needs to try to increase sales or reduce costs at particular times.

This is a Level 1 (1–3 marks) response
Marks awarded – 3 out of 6

b) This is a good answer. James has considered how the bank manager will use the information in the forecast to help make a decision. Examples have been provided to illustrate the points James has made. James has quite correctly identified that the main concern of the bank manager is whether the business will be able to afford to repay the loan. The only thing which James might have been able to add is that the figures in the forecast are only estimates and that there is therefore no guarantee that the figures will be 100% accurate.

This is a Level 3 (7–8 marks) response
Marks awarded – 7 out of 8

Question Five (Common Question)

a) Explain the difference between:
   i)   Gross and Net profit. **(4)**
   ii) Profit and Cash flow. **(4)**
b) Making a Profit is important for most businesses.
   Explain why this is the case. **(8)**

Student Answer

a) i) Gross profit is sales revenue less the cost of goods sold. Net Profit is Gross Profit less expenses. Net profit is the amount of profit left over once the expenses of running the business have been deducted from the Gross Profit.

ii) Profit is the amount of money left over after a business has paid for all the costs of running the business. Cash Flow, on the other hand, is the flow of money into and out of the business over a particular period of time.

b) It is important for a business to make a profit because it is necessary for the business to expand. Without profit, the business would not be able to pay for new equipment. Shareholders will also want the business to make a profit because they will want some of this profit in the form of dividends. If the business does not a make a profit the possibility exists that the business may become insolvent. Profit will allow the business to compete in a market and take advantage of any upturns in the economy.

Laura

What the Examiner Says

a) i) This a good answer both types of profit have been correctly defined to help distinguish between them.
         Marks awarded – 4 out of 4

     ii) Another good answer. Clear definitions have been provided which distinguish between the two terms.
         Marks awarded – 4 out of 4

b) This answer is not as clear as it could have been. There are some relevant statements which are in need of a little more detail and explanation. Laura has included some relevant facts but they are not very clearly explained. There are also some inaccurate statements. It would have been much better had she explained, first, that without a making a profit it would be unlikely that the business would be able to pay its running costs. If this were to be the case, it is highly likely that the business would fail and become insolvent. She has correctly identified that profit is a major source of internal finance for most businesses and that, in Limited companies, there is an expectation by shareholders that they will receive a dividend, in return for investing in the business, based on the profit made. The final statement regarding being able to compete in the economy is irrelevant.

This is a Level 2 (4 – 6 marks) answer
Marks awarded – 5 out of 8

Marketing

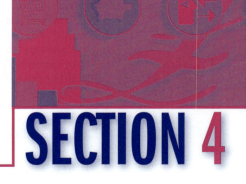

SECTION 4

SOME BASICS

Marketing is **not** just about selling a product or a service. It is the ways in which a business identifies the needs of its customers, produces goods or services that customers want, informs customers about its products or services through advertising and promotions, sets a price that customers will pay, makes sure that the products or services are available when and where customers want, and finally makes sure the customer is satisfied with the level of service given or quality of product received.

When **all** of the above are working well **together**, the business has a successful marketing strategy. Although you will learn the different parts of marketing separately, you need to understand how the different parts outlined above affect each other.

Revision Material

KNOWLEDGE HIERARCHY: MARKETING

This information is intended to provide a quick reminder. Your notes, and the information in the textbook you have used, should provide more detailed information and examples.

Analysing the Market

Topic	Key Features	Detail	Further Information
Market Orientation	• Aimed at consumer	• Used by most businesses	• More sure of success • More costly
Product Orientation	• Producing what business wants	• Used in the past, little used now	• May lead to expensive failures • Avoids cost of market research
Market Segments	• Splits up the market	• Age, gender quality, etc. • Socio-economic Groups	• A, B, C1, C2, D and E or Groups 1 to 5
Identify Disposable Income	• Money left after paying essential bills	• Important for more luxury products and services	
Mass Market	• Aimed at most consumers	• E.g. Ford cars	
Niche Market	• Aimed at a smaller market	• E.g. Ferrari cars	
Test Market	• Marketing in a restricted area	• Helps business trial products before selling to full market	• May save time and money
Market Research – Primary	• Sometimes called field research	• Questionnaires, interviews	• Provides detailed accurate information on products • More costly
		• Sampling	• Quota, random
Primary	• Consumer panels	• Groups used to reporting on products	• Used by larger businesses
Primary	• Testing/observing	• Used in developing food/drink products	• Unsuitable for many products
Market Research – Secondary	• Can be called desk research	• Census, Internet, internal data, trade information	• Cheaper • May not accurately meet business needs
SWOT analysis	• Strengths Weaknesses Opportunities Threats	• Used for new product/activity	• Useful when comparing performance with other businesses
USP analysis	• Unique selling point	• Identifies differences in product/service	• Used in promotions to market the product

The Market Mix

Topic	Key Features	Detail	Further Information
Product	• Product mix/range	• Types of product/ service offered	• May be a budget range and an up-market range
	• Customer needs	• Design	• Size, colour, appeal
	• Branding	• Developing a known name	• E.g. Kellogg's, Sony, Nike, Cadbury
	• Research and development	• Changes to existing products or developing new ones	• Leads to product innovation, e.g. Dyson cleaners
	• Product life cycle	• Introduction Growth Maturity Saturation Decline	• Stages of life cycle affect other parts of market mix
	• Extension strategies	• Adding value, price reduction, re-launch	• Used when product is at maturity stage
Price	• Competition based	• Higher, lower, the same	• Important for new businesses or new products • Higher indicates exclusive, etc.
	• Penetration	• Lower price then higher	• Used to gain market share
	• Skimming/creaming	• Higher price for time when product is new	• Used in high tech products, e.g. games consoles
	• Cost Plus	• Costs plus profit	• Essential if losses to be avoided
	• Differential	• Different prices for same product or service	• Often used in transport
	• Promotional	• Price reduction for short time	• E.g. the January sales
	• Psychological	• £99.99 rather than £100	• Widely used for all types of products
	• Supply	• The business side of marketing	• Amount a business is prepared to sell • Businesses want higher prices
	• Demand	• The consumer side of marketing	• Amount consumers are prepared to buy • Consumers want lower prices

Topic	Key Features	Detail	Further Information
Price *cont.*	• Elasticity	• How demand changes when price changes • Can affect marketing strategies and promotional activities	• Measured in % • Important when considering a change in price
Place	• Direct	• Internet, mail order	• Used by smaller businesses • Not suitable for all products
	• Through retailer or wholesaler	• Shops, catalogues, markets	• Most goods sold this way, e.g. food, clothes, cars
Promotion	• Advertising	• Persuasive, informative	• Persuasive, gives opinions • Informative, gives facts
	• Media	• Television, radio, newspapers, magazines, Internet, billboards, cinema	• Choice depends on cost, type of product, target market to be reached
	• Sales promotions	• BOGOF, added value, loss leader, competitions, free sample, merchandising, guarantees	• Choice depends on product, stage of life cycle, target market
	• Public relations (PR)	• Keeping business in the public eye	• E.g. newspaper stories, magazine articles rather than adverts
	• Sponsorship	• Often used in sport	• E. g. Barclaycard, Nationwide, Embassy, N Power, Zurich

Consumer Protection

Topic	Key Features	Detail	Further information
The Law	• Supply of Goods Act	• Goods are satisfactory quality, as described, fit for purpose	• Money back for consumer if law broken
	• Weights and Measures Act	• Certain products only	• E.g. alcohol sold in certain measures • Enforced by Trading Standards
	• Consumer Protection Acts	• Labelling of dangerous products	• Identifies rights of consumers and responsibilities of retailers
		• Laws on the advertising of sale prices	• Sold for 28 days at previous price
	• Food and Drugs Acts	• Labelling of food, and contents	• E.g. orange juice, orange squash must have certain orange content
		• Who can buy/sell drugs	
	• Consumer Credit Act	• APR must be stated • Credit agreement given to consumer	• Consumer can compare credit terms
	• European Union	• Directives given on food and doorstep selling amongst others	• E.g. colouring allowed in food
Trade organisations	• E.g. Association of British Travel Agents (ABTA)	• Membership is voluntary • Gives consumer confidence	• Compensation if a problem with holiday
Independent organisations	• Consumer's Association • Citizens Advice Bureau	• Produce Which? Magazine	• Independent comparison of products
Government organisations	• 'Watchdogs'	• OFTEL, OFWAT are examples	• Control prices • Influence marketing activity
	• Office of Fair Trading	• Influences mergers and takeovers	• Investigates if mergers, etc. are in the interests of the consumer

PUTTING IT IN CONTEXT

Matt Richards Ltd is a company which makes designer plastic products such as waste-paper bins, pen holders and letter racks. It is a *market orientated* business, always making sure that consumers like a new product before it is developed fully. The managing director of the company, Matt, believes this approach will save the company money, even though it will mean some *market research* has to be carried out.

The market for the company's product is a *niche* one. Matt knows that he is aiming the products at a small market. He feels the business is not big enough to supply goods to a larger *mass market*. The target market for the designer products are 20- to 30-year olds in *socio-economic groups* A, B, and C1 who are prepared to spend rather more money on items for the home that are a little different. These groups, being more wealthy, have a greater *disposable income* to spend on such items.

Matt is now developing a new range of products for the kitchen. His designers have come up with new ideas for food containers and general storage. Matt knows that the next stage will need some detailed *market research*. He decides to ask a business specialising in market research to carry out some *primary research*, conducting *interviews* with the *target market*. The *sample* of people asked is chosen by the *quota* method, as information is only really needed from the top range (A, B and C1) of the *socio-economic* groups.

When a new product range is developed, the company takes the opportunity to conduct a *SWOT* analysis in order to examine their strengths, weaknesses opportunities and threats in relation to the new products. Matt knows that the main *strength* of the business is their unique designs, but recognises that the price is high and this is seen as a *weakness*. There are other businesses which make plastic kitchen containers which is clearly a *threat*, but there are great *opportunities* with the growth in sales of specialist kitchen equipment in recent years. Overall the *USP* (Unique Selling Point) of the business is thought to be the design, and it is thought that this should be the main theme of any future *advertising* for the new products.

When the products were being developed, Matt held a meeting to decide on how the kitchen products should be marketed. The meeting decided to use the *market mix* as a framework for discussion. The business knows that for a successful *marketing strategy*, all parts of the market mix should work together.

There would be a *product mix* of different colours and sizes of containers. The *product life cycle* was thought to be about two years before new designs would be needed.

The *price* would be *competitor*-based, but a little higher to indicate better quality. At first there may be a *promotional pricing* period to introduce the new range. The accountant pointed out that any costs of production, development and marketing must be recovered in the final price, and so cost *plus* pricing should not be ignored.

Success in marketing requires the correct mix

The *advertising* of the product would be in specialist *trade magazines* for the shops who bought the products, and in up-market newspapers with a high A, B and C1 readership. Giving some containers as prizes in television cooking shows was thought to be a good *PR* exercise.

The *place* where the products were sold was discussed at the meeting. The present *method of distribution* was to sell to up-market high street shops, but the marketing manager, Heather, was keen to go into *direct marketing*, selling the new kitchen containers on the *Internet*, and by *mail order*. Heather thought that this would increase profit, as it would cut out the shops. As the products were aimed at more wealthy consumers they would most likely have a computer at home through which to order.

When the marketing material was being put together, the company had to be careful to describe the products accurately; otherwise it would be breaking the *Sale of Goods Act*. Matt also checked to see if any *directives* from the *European Union* affected the manufacture and sale of plastic food containers. He, too, didn't want to break any laws!

 ACTIVITIES

ACTIVITY ONE

Design a questionnaire to find out consumer opinions on a new range of hair shampoo. You should include questions on:

- Price
- Place
- Possible Promotions
- Products
- Any other areas you feel may provide useful information

Your questionnaire must have *at least* 10 questions.

Explain how you will a) identify your sample, b) carry out the questionnaire.

ACTIVITIES *cont.*

Look at another questionnaire designed by a friend. Explain how you might have been able to improve it.

Remember, in a questionnaire you should be aiming to collect information that will enable a business to develop a successful marketing strategy.

ACTIVITY TWO

What *pricing* strategy would be suitable for the following situations? Give reasons for your answer.

Setting the correct price for a product is a complicated process

- A little-known electrical business wants to enter the widescreen television market.
- A famous chocolate maker has developed a new caramel-flavoured snack.
- A car maker has an old model car coming towards the end of its product life cycle.
- A well-known computer games console maker introduces a new revolutionary product, more powerful than any of its competitors.
- An established airline business wants to increase sales. The business has a lot of competitors.

ACTIVITY THREE

1. Complete the following spider diagram to show the methods of promotion that might be used by a national fast-food chain.

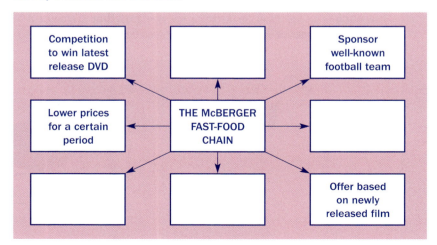

2. Explain why the methods of promotion would be suitable for a national fast food restaurant
3. Complete a similar spider diagram and explanation for Leopard, a car manufacturer wanting to introduce a new, fast sports car

ACTIVITY FOUR

Plan a marketing strategy for a well known drinks company wanting to introduce a new fruit-flavoured soft drink. You have the following further information:

- The target market is 10- to 25-year olds, male and female
- The makers want to emphasise the health qualities of the drink
- A large marketing budget is available

In completing the strategy, **all** aspects of the marketing mix should be covered, emphasising how **each** of the four Ps of the marketing mix work **together** to produce a successful strategy. Your marketing strategy should be between one and two sides of A4 paper.

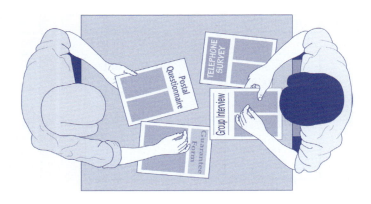

AQA 'A' questions may ask you to give the meaning and examples of terms such as:

- Primary and Secondary Research
- Market Segments
- SWOT and USP Analysis
- The Four Ps of the Market Mix
- The Stages of the Product Life Cycle
- Skimming, Penetration and other pricing strategies
- Direct Marketing
- Point of Sale, Loss Leaders and other methods of sales promotion
- Consumer Protection

More difficult questions you may be asked in either specification 'A' or 'B':

- Explain the suitability of using primary research for a particular situation.
- Evaluate the benefits of using SWOT analysis in a particular situation.
- Explain how the market mix may be applied to different products and services.
- Evaluate the use of different parts of the market mix at different stages of the product life cycle.
- Explain how a business might develop a marketing strategy for a particular product
- Analyse the way in which different promotion techniques are used in different stages of the product life cycle.
- Evaluate the use of Internet-based marketing compared to more traditional High Street stores.
- Explain how and why consumers are protected by law.
- Explain how a business might benefit from using different pricing strategies.

Some examples of these types of questions are given in the following section. Look carefully at what the question is asking you to do; how the student has answered the question; what the examiner thinks of the answer

MARKETING: SPECIMEN QUESTIONS

Question one (Common Question)

a) Explain what is meant by the following pricing strategies:
    i)   Skimming
    ii) Penetration   **(4)**
b) Explain **two** promotion methods a business might use to
    increase sales.   **(4)**

Student Answer

a)   Skimming is where a new product is priced very highly to entice the
      wealthy buyers to buy on the assumption that as it is very expensive and
      new then the product must be of a very good quality and be worth
buying. It can also be said to have a 'prestige' value meaning that it is better than
anything else – very high class/quality.

Penetration pricing is where a company will set a very low price for their product in order to attract a large number of customers and hence increase its market share very quickly as its competitors charge a much higher price for relatively the same product.

b) *A business could increase its sales by advertising the product in question either on TV or radio, or any other forms of media, for that matter. This would increase the number of people that actually know the product exists and if the product is made desirable, whether by its appearance or price, then the potential customer would be enticed into buying the product. Also, as another form of increasing sales, a business could offer free testing of the product, be it a free trial for an Internet supplier or a free sample of a piece of shortbread. This would have the same affect as advertising as it would increase the number of people wanting to buy the product.*

Sarah

What the Examiner Says

a) Sarah has answered this very well, up to a point. She clearly understands that skimming will mean a higher price, which may well mean that a product has a high prestige value. What she has failed to recognise is that skimming has a time span, and that in time the higher price will be reduced as new products come along.

With penetration pricing the same mistake has been made. Yes, the price will be lower to attract customers, but this will increase over time as customers become aware of the brand and product.

Marks awarded – 2 out of 4

b) Sarah has answered this section very well. She has concentrated on two distinct promotion activities, advertising and free trials. These are clearly explained with relevant examples.

Marks awarded – 4 out of 4

Question Two (Higher Tier)

Q

Emotions Ltd makes skincare products.
They concentrate on the teenage market, both boys and girls, and have a new product aimed at the prevention of teenage spots. Recommend a marketing strategy Emotions Ltd might use for this new product. **(12)**

Student Answer

For teenagers it is always worthwhile advertising on TV as that is what most of them watch on a daily basis, also the time is important of the screening of the advert – it needs to be in between a teenage programme – not many teenagers are caught watching 'Countdown'! Also you have to prove that it does work by testing it in the first place and labelling it as dermatologically tested. If you would want them to believe you more you could employ a famous personality that is respected by both sexes, for instance by having David Beckham say that it does work.

Also you would need to make the product desirable, not many teenagers talk about what skincare products they use so it is important not to rely on knowledge of the product being passed around by word-of-mouth and the company would have to count on designing a product that would be sufficiently eye-catching and grab the teenager's attention so that they actually feel like buying it.

Finally, price can be important due to the low budget of a teenager. However, it may be possible that they can just ask their parents to buy it next time they do the weekly family shop. Another idea for the teenagers is offering a free trial-period pack where they can have a free pack that would last them for, let's say, two weeks and if they don't notice a difference then they haven't lost any money. However if the product does work and reduces their spots then they may feel more confident in buying it, as they know for a fact without spending anything that it will work on their face. This would cause profits to be slack at first, but if the product did work then profits should increase dramatically.

Damon

What the Examiner Says

With any question asking for a marketing strategy, the market mix can be used as a framework, but it is *vital* that the answer shows how the market mix works *together* to produce a successful strategy.

Damon has identified advertising, trial packs and endorsement (David Beckham) as part of promotion. Price is seen as an issue, as is the design of the product itself. There is no clear reference to place, i.e. where the product is to be sold and the distribution methods to be used.

Damon has chosen his examples well, indicating where and when the product should be advertised, and the endorsement link is well made. The reference to testing is important in the modern marketplace. The section on price could have been covered in more business-like terms, for example should the business use penetration or skimming methods?

What the answer lacks is how the elements of the market mix will work together. For example the advertising should emphasise the pricing strategy, which will display the characteristics of the product, with a clear distribution plan to ensure that the product is available in outlets that the target market will use (or their parents, as identified by Damon!).

Question Three (Higher Tier)

Quench is a new soft drink made by Fisher Ltd. Quench is to be targeted at adult consumers wanting to keep fit and enjoy a refreshing drink.

Evaluate the different advertising media Fisher Ltd might use for Quench.

(8)

Student Answer

If you want to target a specific audience then Fisher Ltd would need to find out what that specific audience either listens to, reads or watches so that they know where to advertise their new product. It may be that they have to advertise in fitness magazines to attract that particular niche market. Also a good idea would be to have the new drink, Quench, on sale in places that fitness people go to, such as gyms, knowing that they would be thirsty after a good workout and they would have this new drink at hand ready to be bought. If the price is sufficiently tempting it would be highly likely that they would go for Quench over another well-known invigorating drink.

Tracy

What the Examininer Says

Tracy starts her answer well, explaining that Fisher Ltd would certainly have to conduct their own research into their target market. Having said that she chooses an example well, in fitness magazines. The answer then begins to fall away. Whilst the sale of the drink in gyms would also advertise the product, sales and advertising should be separated when answering the question. The reference to price is not required.

The vital element which Tracy has missed is that the command word is *'evaluate'*. This means that she should have examined the different *media* (not the place of sale as such) which Fisher Ltd might use and then judge, giving reasons, which is the most appropriate, in her opinion, for the new soft drink. For example other media include TV, newspapers, cinemas, radio, etc. A number of these could have formed the basis for the evaluation of the most appropriate media for Fisher Ltd to use.

Question Four (Higher Tier)

Q

Coldstream plc make washing machines. At present they only sell to main electrical shops who then sell on to consumers. The marketing manager now feels that they should sell direct to the consumer.

Evaluate the different methods of direct sales, recommending to Coldstream whether they should change to this new method of distribution. **(10)**

Student Answer

If Coldstream wanted to sell direct to the consumer they would have to consider many factors such as marketing their product by themselves, as they sell direct to retailers who normally know what they're doing – if they offer a quality product that is reasonably priced, chances are they would buy your product.

However due to Coldstream wanting to take the retailer out of the equation then they would have to advertise direct to the consumer and in that spend a lot more on advertising. Also profits would reduce in the short term because of the extra costs of advertising a new service. Further costs would come from the setting up of a distribution section and customer service, as the shops would no longer play this role. Consumers will need to see the benefits of direct sales, rather than buying at places such as Currys.

Coldstream also have many other options available to them if they did decide to go ahead with the plan. For instance they could go for mail order instead of opening a shop themselves – this would basically be a consumer ordering direct from the factory. Or Coldstream could go for a factory shop instead of different shops scattered around the country.

A further option would be to sell on the Internet. The company (being a plc) would have a website already and so the extra cost of setting up a sales page would be minimal

My opinion is that Coldstream should make a compromise at first and operate an Internet system that would stretch out to the entire country (at minimal cost) while at the same time having a shop in the factories. If this is found to be a success then they may choose to expand further and open separate shops themselves around the country, and set up a mail order business. There will be costs in the short term for the new service but in the long run I feel that the direct sales will work, providing the product is good and the price is attractive to consumers.

Ben

What the Examiner Says

This question falls into two parts, the evaluation of direct sales methods, and whether direct selling should be adopted by Coldstream plc.

Ben covers both parts well. He identifies various direct selling methods (Internet, mail order, factory shops) and recognises that costs will be involved with them all, though the Internet approach is favoured as the addition to an existing website will keep costs down.

Problems associated with direct selling are dealt with very well. The cost of setting up such a system, including advertising, customer services, etc. are covered in some detail.

The judgement at the end of the answer is well made, looking at a gradual approach to the change, whist recognising that there must be a quality product at an attractive price to tempt consumers away from more traditional outlets such as Currys.

This is a top Level 3 (8–10 marks) answer, with Ben being awarded full marks.

Question Five (Common Question)

a) Explain how government 'watchdogs' such as OFTEL help protect the consumer **(4)**

b) Explain **two** other ways in which the consumer is protected when buying goods and services. **(4)**

Student Answer

a) OFTEL is responsible for the phone industry, be it the mobile phone industry or cable or privatised phones. OFTEL is always regulating the prices of calls and ensuring that the customer is fairly treated.

b) A consumer can usually take a product back, if he/she still has the receipt for the product. This may be because they are not happy with the product or that there is something wrong with the product itself. Also a customer is protected by the Office of Fair Trading in general, which ensures that the consumer is not treated in an offensive way and is given a fair deal for a product and not 'ripped off'.

Kirsty

What the Examiner Says

a) Kirsty has concentrated on OFTEL, though the question is not specifically set on that particular regulator. She has recognised the role in price setting, though this is not developed. The customer being 'fairly treated' is too vague. What is required is an explanation of minimum service requirements and the regulation of price related to, for example, the rate of inflation.

Marks awarded – 1 out of 4

b) The ability of a consumer to take goods back is covered, although Kirsty has *not* stated the law that relates to this (Sale of Goods). It is the *law* in this instance which protects the consumer.

The second example given by Kirsty is the Office of Fair Trading. This example however is not fully explained. The 'ripped off' comment is too vague to be given a mark. What is required for this example is an explanation of the role of the Office of Fair Trading protecting the consumer from problems relating to the monopoly power of businesses.

Marks awarded – 2 out of 4

Production

SOME BASICS

A firm breaks even when sales revenue equal costs

All businesses must carefully monitor their costs, both variable and fixed. Costs should always be less than revenue in the long term in order to provide a profit. Where total costs equal total revenue, a business is said to break even. The calculation of break-even is useful for a business in order that it knows the number of products it needs to sell, or the value of services it needs to provide, before it makes a profit. The calculation itself, however, may not always be useful for a business.

A business may grow in many ways, by integrating with other businesses or simply growing by itself. The growth of a business may bring benefits such as economies of scale, and an ability to change the method of production it has used. Quality and productivity are essential if a business is to remain competitive.

Revision Material

This information is intended to provide a quick reminder. Your notes, and the information in the textbook you have used, should provide more detailed information and examples.

Costs, Revenue and Break-Even

Topic	Key Features	Detail	Further Information
Costs	• Fixed costs	• Do not change with level of production	• E.g. Rent, Business Rates
	• Variable costs	• Change with level of production	• E.g. Materials
	• Total costs	• Fixed costs plus variable costs	
	• Average costs	• Total costs divided by number sold	• Helps to set price
Revenues	• Sales revenue	• Quantity sold multiplied by selling price	• Often called sales turnover
Break-Even	• Where total costs equal total revenue	• No profit or loss is made	
	• Contribution	• Selling price minus variable cost per unit	
	• Formula for calculation of break-even	• Total fixed costs divided by contribution	• May be used to decide on price levels
	• Margin of safety	• The amount by which sales are more than the break-even level	• Often confused with profit
	• Limitations of use	• All forecasts are liable to change	• Costs of business might change
		• Assumption that all production is sold	
		• Activities of competitors might change	• Competitors may lower their prices
	• Benefits of use	• Helps plan ahead • Production levels and market price can be identified • Often a minimum aim of a business	• Often used when business is new or launching a new product

Types and Scale of Production

Topic	Key Features	Detail	Further Information
Scale of Production	• Capacity of a business	• Above capacity	• Producing more than the resources should be capable of doing
		• Below capacity	• Producing less than the business should be capable of doing
Business Growth	• Economies of scale	• Unit cost reduced as production increases	
		• Purchasing	• Discount for buying goods in bulk
		• Managerial	• Specialist managers improve performance
		• Financial	• Cost of raising finance is less
		• Marketing	• Savings on advertising and distribution
		• Risk bearing	• Firm not dependent on one product
		• Technical	• Firm can buy the most efficient machinery
	• Diseconomies of scale	• Unit costs increase as production increases	• Problems with communication and control
Integration	• Merger	• Two or more firms agree to join	• Can be agreed or hostile where no agreement
	• Takeover	• A firm buying the control of another	• May be subject to government approval
	• Internal growth	• A firm growing on its own	
	• Vertical	• Forwards vertical	• E.g. Furniture maker takes over furniture shop
		• Backwards vertical	• E.g. Furniture maker takes over wood supplier
	• Horizontal	• A firm joining with another firm involved in the same business	• Furniture maker joins with another furniture maker

Topic	Key Features	Detail	Further Information
Integration *cont.*	• Diversification	• A firm joining with another firm in a different business	• Furniture maker joins with travel business
Measuring Business Size	• Sales	• The total value of goods sold	• May be a small firm but selling high cost items, e.g. jewellery
	• Market share	• The % of a total market a firm controls	• Often used in car industry
	• Number of employees	• Can be a problem with capital intensive firms	
Methods of Production	• Job	• Each product individually produced	• E.g. Handmade furniture
	• Batch	• A number of products made at the same time	• E.g. Loaves of bread
	• Flow	• Made on an assembly line	• E.g. Cars. Work often repetitive
Division of Labour	• Each worker concentrates on one job	• Less training • Quicker completion • More efficient use of time • Can lead to boredom	• Often used in flow production • Lack of motivation if work is very repetitive
Technology and Production	• CAD	• Computer aided design	• Saves time and expensive testing
	• CAM	• Computer aided manufacture	• Less labour needed. Saves costs in long term
	• CIM	• Computer integrated manufacture	• All the business is computer controlled

Productivity and Quality Control

Topic	Key Features	Detail	Further Information
Productivity	• Producing more per worker	• Involves greater flexibility from workers	• Can lead to problems between management and workers
	• Lean production	• Cutting down on all production costs • Includes JIT (Just In Time) methods	• Reduces stock • Saves storage costs
Quality Control	• Japanese methods • May be a separate department	• Include Kaizan, Kan–ban	• Influence on industry
	• Total Quality Management (TQM)	• All workers involved	• Workers responsible for quality of their own work

PUTTING IT IN CONTEXT

Tim and Mel are partners trading as Devilish Stagewear. Tim has experience as a keyboard player in a band and his partner Mel was a seamstress making clothing for a number of years. They feel there is a market for specialist stagewear aimed at the growing number of amateur and professional bands.

Both Tim and Mel are aware of their *costs*. As they operate from home they hope to minimise their *fixed costs* such as *rent* and *business rates*, though the expensive *material* costs for the stagewear will make up a large proportion of their *variable costs*. *Revenue* will come from the sales of the outfits Mel produces, which in the first six months of the business were above the *break-even* figure required. Projected sales for the next six months are higher, taking the business further into the *margin of safety*.

The partners are aware that their calculations, such as *break-even*, may not always be accurate. Tim wonders whether other businesses may start with the same ideas on making stagewear and possibly take some of their custom. Mel is more concerned at the price of the material she has to buy, as she knows that a future price rise will severely affect their calculations. There is no real scope for *computer aided manufacture*, the business is too small, though Mel sees *computer aided design* as a help to produce eye catching stagewear.

Producing *quality* goods is vital for Tim and Mel if they are to gain a good reputation and secure further orders. They plan to operate on a *Total Quality Management* approach, with each worker being responsible for the quality of their own work. Tim is responsible for the quality of the administration and sales service, Mel being responsible for the quality of the stagewear she makes. The partnership will operate their own *Just-In-Time* method of production, with materials arriving only when needed. This will save the business *costs* of holding expensive *stock* of specialist material.

The partners hope that the business will grow in the future, and so be able to take advantage of *economies of scale*. Mel will be able to buy the material she needs in *bulk*, and more advanced sewing machinery to speed up manufacture. This will help reduce the costs of the business. Any future growth is expected to be *internal* (there are no other businesses concentrating on stagewear), though there is the possibility of some *diversification* if Tim develops his electrical experience and produces electrical safety equipment for bands and clubs.

 # ACTIVITIES

ACTIVITY ONE

Sarah Langley owns Floral Art, specialising in quality flower arrangements. Below is a list of some of her costs:

- Rent
- Business Rates
- Flowers for the arrangements
- Bank loan
- An advertisement every week in the local paper
- Ribbons for the arrangements
- Business cards
- Postage

Put each of the costs into the correct column in your own copy of the chart similar to the one below.

Fixed Costs	Variable Costs

ACTIVITY TWO

The following are definitions of terms used in connection with break-even. What is the name of the term to which each definition refers?

a) The difference between the break-even level of output and a higher level of output at which a profit is made.
b) Selling price minus the variable costs per unit.
c) Where total costs equal total revenue.
d) Costs which rise and fall with the level of production.
e) The money received from sales.
f) Costs which remain the same when the level of production changes.

Draw a break-even chart and show each of the terms in the correct position on the chart.

ACTIVITY THREE

Nazish and Rachael want to start a business making picture frames. They have identified the following costs for their business.

Cost	Amount
Rent and Business Rates	£100 per week
Materials per frame	£2.50
Other variable costs per frame	£3.50

They expect to sell each frame for £10.

a) Calculate the number of frames that Nazish and Sarah must sell per week in order to break even.

b) Draw a break-even chart to show the break-even position of the business.

c) Using the break-even chart, or further calculations, show how the break-even amount would change if the price they charged per frame was:
   i)   Increased to £16
   ii)   Decreased to £8

ACTIVITY FOUR

Below are features connected with the growth of businesses. Expand the diagram below as far as you can to explain how each feature affects business activity. A start has been made for you (for example there are more economies of scale, etc.). Look to show what each box can lead to. Use a LARGE piece of paper!

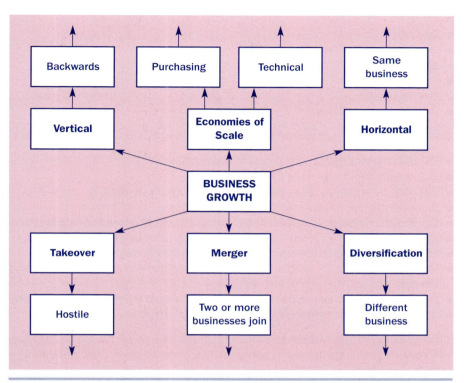

Backwards | Purchasing | Technical | Same business

Vertical | Economies of Scale | Horizontal

BUSINESS GROWTH

Takeover | Merger | Diversification

Hostile | Two or more businesses join | Different business

ACTIVITY FIVE

From your local area, find examples of businesses which use the following methods of production:

- Job
- Batch
- Flow

For **each** business, explain:

a) How the production method works in practice.
b) Why the production method is suited to the business, stating the advantages and disadvantages of this method over the production methods not used.

QUESTION TYPES TO EXPECT

AQA 'A' questions may ask you to give the meaning and examples of such terms as:

- *Fixed and Variable costs*
- *Break-even*

- *Economies of Scale*
- *Diseconomies of Scale*
- *Integration: Vertical, Horizontal, Diversification*
- *Merger*
- *Takeover*
- *Job, Batch and Flow Production*
- *CAD, CAM and CIM*
- *Productivity*
- *Lean Production*
- *Total Quality Management*

More difficult questions you may be asked in both AQA specification 'A' and specification 'B':

- *Calculate the total and average costs from figures provided.*
- *Calculate the break-even using a formula.*
- *Calculate the break-even using data from a table of figures provided.*
- *Draw and interpret a break-even graph to analyse the position of a business.*
- *Explain how a break-even calculation may be either useful or misleading for a business.*
- *Evaluate the economies of scale that may benefit a business in given circumstances.*
- *Analyse and evaluate the different methods of production available to a business.*
- *Identify and evaluate the benefits and problems associated with business growth through integration.*
- *Evaluate the benefits and problems of introducing improved technology within a business.*
- *Analyse and evaluate the benefits of a quality control system in a business.*

Some examples of these types of questions and student answers are given in the following section. Look carefully at what the question is asking you to do; how the student has answered the question; what the examiner thinks of the answer

PRODUCTION: SPECIMEN QUESTIONS

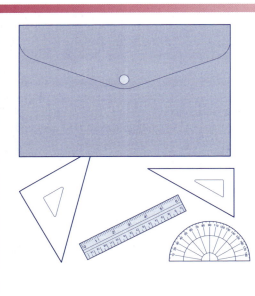

Question One (Higher Tier)

Bendit Ltd makes plastic rulers and other plastic stationery equipment. The weekly production costs for rulers are as follows:

Item	Cost
Plastic per ruler	2p
Other variable costs per ruler	3p
Rent	£250
Business Rates	£125

Bendit Ltd sells the rulers for 55p.

a) Using the data above, calculate the number of rulers Bendit Ltd must sell per week to break even. Show your working. **(4)**

b) Evaluate the benefits and problems of using break-even analysis for a business such as Bendit Ltd. **(8)**

Student Answer

a) Break-even = $\dfrac{\text{Fixed costs}}{\text{Selling price} - \text{Variable costs}}$

$= \dfrac{£250 + £175}{55p - (2p + 3p)}$

$= \dfrac{£425}{50p}$

$= 850$ rulers per week to break even

b) Break-even is useful for a business because the business can plan ahead. It can plan the production levels necessary not only to break even but also move into the margin of safety and so be more certain of making a profit. Break-even also enables the business to see the effect of different prices for its products on the production levels to break even. The higher the price the fewer products need to be sold to break even.

The problems with break-even are that the business does not know if costs will change in the future. This will affect the break-even amount. Also competitors may change their prices, taking custom from the business and so affecting the break-even calculation.

Chris

What the Examiner Says

a) This is a very well set out answer. It is easy to follow how Chris has worked and it is accurate. Even if Chris had made a mistake in his final calculation he would have still been awarded some marks because of his understanding of which figures to use.

Marks awarded – 4 out of 4

b) Chris has explained very well the benefits and problems of using break-even. What he has not done is *evaluated* the benefits and problems. For example do the benefits make it worthwhile for a business to calculate breakeven, given the fact that there are problems? Or are the problems so great that completing a break-even calculation is a waste of time?

Chris might have achieved a Level 1 (1–4 marks) answer worth 4 out of the 8 marks available. Evaluation would have been necessary to achieve a Level 2 (5–8 marks) answer.

Question Two (Common Question)

Q

Longden Ltd prints books and magazines. It is considering taking over a competitor business Cropley Ltd, which also print books and magazines.

a) What type of integration is the proposed takeover of Cropley Ltd by Longden Ltd? **(1)**

b) Explain the benefits of this type of integration to Longden Ltd. **(6)**

Student Answer

a) This type of integration is called horizontal.

b) The benefits of this type of integration is that the business will be much bigger, which will make it much better. It can buy things in bulk which is much better than if you only bought a small amount. If you only bought a small amount then it will cost a lot more than if you bought a large amount, so this will be much better for Longden Ltd.

Sam

What the Examiner Says

a) Sam has correctly identified the takeover as being horizontal.

Marks awarded – 1 out of 1

b) In this section Sam seems to lose her way. She says little which is wrong, correctly identifying that the larger business will indeed be able to buy products at a lower price. This is really where her answer stops. She could have developed her answer to say that the lower price for paper and ink (it is a printing business) will help the business by reducing costs and so increase profits. This is only part of economies of scale. Other parts include technical, managerial and financial benefits (see Knowledge Hierarchy). Sam could also have explained how taking over a competitor business will give Longden Ltd a larger market share, and possibly be able to increase prices which again will help profits.

Marks awarded – 1 out of 6

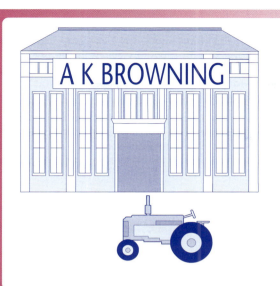

Question Three (Higher Tier)

AK Browning plc make tractors. The tractors are finally assembled on a production line, using flow method of production. Many of the different parts used on each tractor are made by batch methods of production.

Evaluate the benefits of using different methods of production for the final assembly of the tractors and the making of the different parts. **(10)**

Student Answer

Making tractors is like making cars. They will move down on a conveyor belt and parts will be added to others to make the tractor. This is flow production. It is better than job and batch because:

- *It saves training workers and the costs involved. Each job is simple and repetitive. Job production means specialist workers who are highly trained (and so expensive to employ)*
- *A large amount can be made. Making an individual tractor (Job) will be slower and more expensive.*
- *Better use can be made of modern production methods such as robots and other computer controlled machinery. With job and batch production some machinery would be left idle for periods of time.*

Batch production is better for the tractor parts because:

- *The parts will be identical. They can be made by setting up a machine to make the number required. The machine settings will then be changed to make, for example, a different sized part. This saves time and money for the business.*
- *Job production is no good for the parts because job means creating a unique product. The parts are not unique*
- *Flow is no real use for the parts as you wouldn't have a nut and bolt being made on a production line.*

Steve

Question 4 (Common Question)

AJ Computers Ltd make computers for sale by mail order direct to the public. The business uses Total Quality Management throughout its operations.

a) Explain what is meant by Total Quality Management. **(2)**
b) Analyse the problems and benefits of introducing a Total Quality Management system into a business such as AJ Computers Ltd. **(6)**

Student Answer

a) *Total Quality Management is when a business puts great importance on quality and everything is checked to make sure it is of the correct quality.*
b) *The problems of introducing Total Quality Management is that people have to do more work to check the quality and they might not want the extra work. The benefits are that with better quality more people will buy the computers.*

Kevin

What the Examiner Says

a) Here Kevin has recognised that quality will be checked throughout the business (1 mark) but he has failed to say that in Total Quality Management *each* worker is responsible for the quality of their *own* work.

Marks awarded – 1 out of 2

b) The problem of workers having more work to complete is covered by Kevin. He could have written about the cost of training the workers to check for quality which would have been a further problem for the business. As for the benefits, it is true that the business may well sell more computers if quality was improved, though this point should have been developed further to include a possible rise in profits and bonus payments for workers if production and sales reached a particular level. Another point which could have been made is the *necessity* to improve quality to keep up with competitors, especially in a business such as computers where there are many suppliers. Kevin's answer is a good illustration of student's work which has said nothing wrong, but failed to gain even half marks.

Marks awarded – 2 out of 6

People and Organisations

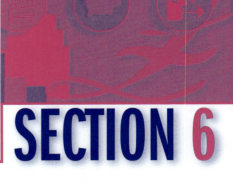

SECTION 6

SOME BASICS

People can make organisations successful – or otherwise. Organisations must recruit and select workers. The process involves identifying the needs of the business, advertising the post and then gathering information about the applicants to decide who to employ. Many organisations provide extensive training for their workers in order to develop their skills and to raise productivity. They also use motivation techniques to make sure workers work to their best. These motivational techniques may involve pay but there are other ways that do not involve any payment. Finally, there are laws that organisations must obey when they employ workers. Many of these are designed to protect workers from unscrupulous employers.

Revision Material

KNOWLEDGE HIERARCHY: LIST OF THINGS TO KNOW ABOUT THE EXTERNAL ENVIRONMENT OF BUSINESS

This information is intended to provide a quick reminder. Your notes, and the information in the textbook you have used, should provide more detailed information and examples.

Topic	Key Features	Detail	Further Information
Recruitment and Selection	• Needs Analysis	• Job Description • Person Specification	• Tasks, duties • Qualifications, qualities, skills
	• Advertising the job	• Media	• Internal or external • Local/national newspapers/radio • Specialist magazines • Internet • Job centres • Word of mouth

Topic	Key Features	Detail	Further information
Recruitment and Selection *cont*.		• Factors influencing which media used	• Cost of media • Wealth of firm • Type of worker • Location of job • Number of workers needed
	• Selecting the worker	• Sources of information	• CV • Letter of application • Application form • Interview • Reference • Test • Presentations
Pay and Motivation	• Pay methods	• Hourly rate, overtime • Salary • Profit sharing • Piece rate • Commission • Bonuses • Fringe benefits	• Pay per item made • Percentage of sales • Reaching a target • Discounts on goods, etc.
	• Non-pay methods	• Job rotation • Job enlargement • Job enrichment • Team working • Award schemes • Promotion • Leadership types	• Varying the work • Adding to the job • Giving responsibility • E.g. worker of the month • Autocratic • Laissez-faire • Democratic
Training	• Needs	• New skills • Product knowledge • Group working • Flexibility	• Management • Personal • Technical
	• Types of training	• Re-training • On-the-job • Off-the-job	• Lectures • Simulations • Demonstrations • Team-building
Employment Laws and Trade Unions	• Main laws	• Equal pay • Race Discrimination	

Topic	Key Features	Detail	Further information
Employment Laws and Trade Unions *cont.*	• Main laws *cont.*	• Sex Discrimination • Health and Safety • Minimum Wage • Employment Rights	• Contract of employment
	• Benefits of unions	• Pay • Hours • Working conditions • Holidays • Unfair dismissal • Redundancy	
	• Strength of a union	• Numbers • Wealth • Type of worker • Industrial action	• Skilled vs unskilled • Strikes • Overtime ban • Work to rule

PUTTING IT IN CONTEXT

Grosvenor Lodge is a health farm in Rawcliffe. It employs 40 people. There are fitness instructors, beauticians, masseurs, nutritionists, office staff, cleaners and a handyman.

Grosvenor Lodge needs to employ two additional beauticians. The General Manager, Martin Barness, who deals with *personnel* issues has drawn up a *job description* so that he is clear about the tasks that they will have to carry out and *a person specification* that describes the qualifications, skills and experience for which they are looking. To attract appropriately skilled applicants Martin included some of this information in the *advertisement*. The advertisement asked for beauticians. Grosvenor Lodge really needed two female beauticians to balance the team but Martin knew it was against *equal opportunities laws* to specify female beauticians. He advertised externally in a local newspaper because the job would only interest local people, it was fairly cheap and he was confident there would be local people available. Martin interviewed a *shortlist* of five applicants.

Martin also observed each of the short-listed beauticians giving treatment so that he could assess if they had the knowledge and skills to deal with the customers.

The newly appointed beauticians were given a one-day *induction course* to introduce them to the business – its aims and objectives, the

Tests help to see if the workers have the right skills

premises and the people they would work with. Along with the other beauticians, the two new recruits also took part in a *health and safety* training session after normal hours. Martin hoped that this would prevent any accidents at work which could lead to Grosvenor Lodge being sued by one of its employees or failing a health and safety inspection because staff were not following proper procedures.

All the beauticians are *paid by the hour*. The pay is well above the *minimum national wage*. They can earn additional pay at one and half times the normal hourly rate by working *overtime* or at the weekends. To motivate the workers to provide a quality service that will maintain existing clients and attract new customers, Grosvenor Lodge also runs a *profit-sharing scheme*. Twenty-five per cent of the annual profits are shared out amongst all the employees. There is also an *Employee of the Month* Award. The worker who gains the most of these in a year receives a *bonus*. All the workers are in *teams* – the beauticians make up one team. They meet once a month to discuss any matters that concern them. Sometimes they discuss pay and conditions of work. In the three years since Grosvenor Lodge was started, the management has always responded positively to ideas and problems brought to them by the team representatives. The workers do not feel that they need to join a *trade union* to give them more influence.

 # ACTIVITIES

ACTIVITY ONE
Draw a flow chart to show the sequence of events that are likely to take place in the process of recruitment and selection of a new employee.

ACTIVITY TWO
Match up the worker with an appropriate payment method of motivation.

Worker	Payment Method of Motivation
a) Professional footballer	i) Piece rate
b) Shop assistant	ii) Profit related pay
c) General Manager of a factory	iii) Basic pay plus bonuses
d) Potter making individual pieces	iv) Commission

ACTIVITY THREE
Draw a 'consequence diagram' to show how health and safety laws affect organisations. It should show what might happen in the event of an accident leading to a claim for compensation from an employee.

ACTIVITY FOUR
Draw an image chain that represents the different types of training that a worker may receive:

Worker appointed as new recruit ⟶ worker receives technical training to develop new skills worker job shadows a manager ⟶ worker undertakes simulation training to learn how to deal with problem workers ⟶ worker studies at night school to gain extra qualifications.

Use pictures and captions to indicate the type of training, e.g. on or off the job, induction, the purpose of the training and so on.

ACTIVITIES *cont.*

ACTIVITY FIVE

Write a story of an imaginary or real dispute between workers represented by a trade union and their managers. Discuss what the dispute is about; what actions the union could use; what actions the employers could use; the role of ACAS or an Employment Tribunal in the dispute.

(NB You can research disputes for ideas – try the newspaper websites.)

QUESTION TYPES TO EXPECT

AQA 'A' knowledge questions may ask you to give the meaning and examples of terms such as:

- Job descriptions and person specifications
- Internal and external recruitment.
- CVs, application forms, letters of application, interviews, tests.
- On and off the job training.
- Methods of pay – hourly rates, piece rates, commission etc.
- Non-pay methods of motivation – job rotation, job enrichment, team working etc.
- Laws affecting the employment of workers such as equal pay, race discrimination etc.

Both 'A' and 'B' specifications may ask questions that ask you to make recommendations or judgements. Examples include:

- What information should be included in a job advertisement?
- What media could be used for job advertisements, depending on the type of job, location of work, how much money the firm can afford, etc?
- What methods of selection are appropriate for particular types of workers – CVs or application forms, interviews or presentations, etc?
- Consider the suitability of different pay and non-pay methods of motivating different kinds of workers – piece rates or commission, profit sharing or bonuses.
- What training is appropriate to different kinds of workers or workers in different circumstances?
- How does an employer judge when different labour laws apply – equal pay or race discrimination? Evaluate the consequences of an event or situation.
- What are the benefits of trade union membership, single union agreements.

PEOPLE IN BUSINESS: SAMPLE QUESTIONS

Question One (Higher Tier)

Burnside Engineering plc is based in Preston. It makes components for car engines. The firm needs to recruit two workers. The first is a clerical assistant. The assistant will type letters and keep records of invoices sent and paid using a computer. The second worker is a Marketing Manager who will be responsible for the marketing of the product within the European Union.

Recommend the methods of recruitment and selection that should be used in each of these appointments. Give reasons for your recommendations. **(12)**

Student Answer

The firm needs to draw up a job description and a person specification. The former will give the title of the post, any grade it is rated at, who the worker will be responsible to and the job tasks will all be stated here. The person specification looks at the type of person required and will state whether qualifications, experience, skills and any special requirements such as a valid driving licence are necessary or desirable. In this example, it is very likely that the person specifications will differ greatly as the Marketing Manager will require more qualifications and skills than a clerical assistant.

Now the firm will be ready to advertise the post. They must design each job advert carefully and they may include a selection of the following facts: a description of the job, the qualifications needed, skills needed, experience needed, salary details, hours of work, a contact number and/or future prospects at the firm so that they attract appropriate applicants. The firm must now decide whether to advertise the post internally or externally. An internally advertised post means that someone within the company will step up to the job. I would recommend this for the clerical assistant as it is a relatively small job and it is likely that someone within the company would fill this position. The advantage of employing internally is that the person will already be known to the company and so will not need a long time to adjust to their surroundings. The job could be advertised on a staff notice board or e-mailed internally to those believed to be suitable. However, for the Marketing Manager post I would recommend advertising externally due to a number of reasons. For such an important role it is likely that a person with new ideas will need to be brought in, perhaps with experience of running such an important sector.

*Due to the importance of the skills required, I would recommend advertising in a national newspaper such as **The Times** or **Telegraph** where a suitable audience would read it. A specialist magazine or radio would also be suitable. However the cost of advertising in the first mentioned can be expensive so the latter two may be more suitable, even though they reach a lesser target audience.*

When all the applicants have applied for the post, the company will then wish to draw up a shortlist of the most suitable applicants. It may first look at a letter of application which will clearly highlight the communication skills of the applicant. An application form can be used; this will help the firm to make comparisons between applicants as they will all display the same information. Finally a CV, which the applicant supplies, will also be of benefit as it is their life story displayed at a glance. I would recommend using all of these sources as they will provide a clear view of the ability and qualities of the candidates.

When the suitable candidates have been filtered out, the short list of candidates can be tested for their computer skills (for the clerical assistant) and an interview could take place which will show how well the candidate presents himself or herself. The applicant for the Marketing Manager may also be asked to give a presentation to show how well their skills are developed in this area and the ideas they have to take the firm forward.

From here the most suitable applicant for each job can be selected.

Adam

Question Two (Common Question)

Jim Smith works for Prenton's Electricals Ltd. He solders electrical circuits on to circuit boards. He is paid by piece rate.

a) Explain what is meant by the term 'piece rate'. **(2)**

b) Explain why some businesses may use piece rate to pay some of their workers, but not all of them. **(4)**

c) Recommend **one** method involving pay that Prenton's Electricals Ltd could use for motivating the sales people that it employs. Give reasons for your recommendations. **(4)**

d) Recommend **one** method that does not involve pay that Prenton's could use to motivate the twelve office workers that it employs. Give reasons for your recommendations. **(4)**

Student Answer

a) *Piece rate means that the worker is paid according to how many pieces or items they actually make. This means that the more they make, the more they will be paid.*

b) *Firms like Prenton's Electricals Ltd pay some workers a piece rate because it will motivate workers to make more because they will earn more for themselves and the business. They don't pay all the workers piece rate because they could not pay people in an office this way because they are not making anything that makes a profit.*

c) *Giving the sales people commission for every sale they make will motivate them to sell more products.*

d) *They could arrange staff days out, nights out and even little mini-breaks. This would motivate the office worker.*

Hayley

What the Examiner Says

a) Hayley explains clearly what is meant by the term and what this means to the worker.

Marks awarded 2 out of 2

b) Hayley explains why a business may wish to pay piece rates – in order to make its workers work harder and to gain benefit for the business. She is also fairly clear on how this form of payment is not appropriate for everyone in a business. To gain full marks, she should have explained that piece rates are not appropriate for those workers where it is difficult to calculate their individual contribution to the business. She has actually confused this with profitability.

Marks awarded 3 out of 4

c) Hayley correctly identifies that commission will motivate sales people. Again she does not fully explain what it is and how it encourages sales people. The key phrase is 'percentage of sales revenue'.

Marks awarded – 2 out of 4

d) The suggestion about nights out might work but there is no attempt to explain why this would motivate the office workers. Hayley could have developed the answer by referring to Maslow's hierarchy of needs, explaining how workers may respond positively as a result of their social needs being met. Of course there were other possible answers – worker of the month award schemes, job rotation or enlargement or enrichment. The key to a good score is to apply them to the context and explain how they would work.

Marks awarded – 1 out of 4

Question Three (Common Question)

Johnson's Chemicals Ltd specialises in the disposal of dangerous chemicals.

a) Explain **two** ways in which Johnson's Chemicals Ltd will be affected by employment laws. **(8)**

b) Johnson's Chemicals Ltd has a new worker who will handle the chemicals during the disposal process. Recommend whether the firm should use on-the-job or off-the-job training to train the worker. **(6)**

Student Answer

a) *Sex discrimination – This is when males or females are treated differently because of their sex. This is a law to prevent this happening, e.g. when advertising a job.*

Health and Safety – This law makes it the responsibility of the employer to protect workers from dangers in the work place.

b) *I think the workers should do off-the-job training because it is too dangerous to train on the job because of the dangerous chemicals that would be around. If you did not know what you were doing it could be very dangerous.*

Rashid

What the Examiner Says

a) AQA will not ask questions requiring knowledge of specific Acts of Parliament and dates. Rashid shows that he knows what the laws are about – sex discrimination and health and safety – and would be given credit for this. For another mark connected with sex discrimination, he could have explained what might happen if the business broke the law or he could have discussed exceptional cases when males and females can be treated differently. I would have given two marks for the answer about health and safety, the second mark being for clearly identifying that it is the responsibility of the employer. For further marks, I would like to have seen Rashid discuss health and safety inspections and/or how an employee can sue the business in the event of an accident that is caused by the firm's negligence which could lead to a compensation payment.

Marks awarded – 5 out of 8

b) Again Rashid makes valid points but does not explain them fully. He could have developed an explanation of how off-the-job training would prepare someone in a safe environment, perhaps through simulations dealing with safe materials, before allowing them to handle dangerous materials in a real work situation. He could also have explained how an untrained person in a dangerous situation might do more harm than good. Finally, Rashid could have discussed the likelihood that health and safety regulations would require off-the-job training before the workers were allowed to handle chemicals in the workplace.

Marks awarded – 2 out of 6

Question Four (a) Common Question b) Higher Tier)

Salim Malik works at Birkenhead Ship Builders. He is a member of the trade union.

a) With what problems might the trade union help workers like Salim? **(4)**

b) Explain why the trade union may be better at dealing with Salim's problems than he would be on his own. **(6)**

Student Answer

a) *The trade union may help Salim if he is unfairly dismissed. It may help workers who are unhappy with pay, hours or working conditions in their job. They would also appeal if that member were made redundant. They would make sure workers had a safe environment and they would get the holiday time they needed. Some of the Acts of Parliament that could be abused are sex and race discrimination.*

b) *Because it is not just one person but a body of members. The employers would be under more pressure to fulfil their demands. They offer expert advice and support because they employ specialists such as solicitors who will know what to do. They can fund expensive court cases, they employ trained negotiators who will know how to deal with the employer in question.*

Josephine

What the Examiner Says

These are two very well developed answers.

a) Josephine names eight issues with which a trade union might deal for a member.

Marks awarded – 4 out of 4

b) Josephine discusses several ways in which the union is likely to have more influence than a single individual. It would also have been possible to score well by developing the 'strength through numbers' line of argument – the possibility of disruption through industrial action such as strikes, etc. and the effect of these on the competitiveness and profitability of the firm.

Marks awarded – 6 out of 6

The Changing Business Environment

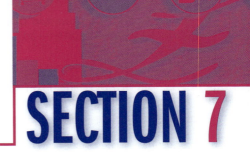

SOME BASICS

An increasing number of businesses sell to, or buy from, other countries. This growth of international trade has meant that the value of a currency, such as the £, becomes more important in decision-making. Profit can be seriously affected if a wrong decision is made and the exchange rate of a currency changes.

The Single Market created opportunity for increased trade with Europe

There has also been a great debate in business circles regarding the merits of being a member of the European Union, and whether to join the Single European Currency – The Euro. There are arguments on both sides; you will need to keep up-to-date with developments. What **is** certain is that international trade, in whatever form, will increase and that businesses must realise that competition can come from anywhere in the world. In some instances international trade must take place if a country requires certain products, e.g. Britain needs to import rice and bananas.

An enlarged European market will cause problems for inefficient businesses

The factors affecting business location have also changed in recent years. Incentives from both the UK government and the EU are persuading some businesses to locate in certain areas of high unemployment, though the 'older' factors of location such as transport and market are still important.

The growing number of larger businesses caused by mergers and takeovers has meant that the government takes a keen interest in making sure that the new monopolies do not act against the interests of the consumer. Mergers need not mean a monopoly being created which operates against the public interest. It may simply mean a larger business being created.

Revision Material

This information is intended to provide a quick reminder. Your notes, and the information in the textbook you have used, should provide more detailed information and examples.

The European Union and International Trade

Topic	Key Features	Detail	Further Information
Why International Trade Takes Place	• Saves costs	• Production in lowest cost countries	• Production spread worldwide
	• Geographic reasons	• Certain products need particular climate	• E.g. Fruit such as bananas
		• Raw materials only in certain places	• E.g. Diamonds
	• Consumer choice	• Consumers like to have wider choice	• Consumers now used to goods from all over the world
	• Political reasons	• May be to support another country or area	• E.g. The Commonwealth countries
Benefits of International Trade to Business	• Larger market	• More countries mean more consumers	• Spreads risk
	• More profit	• Greater sales give opportunity to increase profit	• Increased opportunity with more sales
	• Economies of scale	• Increased production will lower unit costs	• Opportunity to sell at lower prices
Problems of international Trade to Business	• Loss of jobs	• Foreign goods imported mean fewer homemade products made	• E.g. Clothing industry
	• Effect on infant industries	• New industry cannot grow	• Country may be unable to grow economically
	• More competition	• More overseas business selling in UK	• Inefficient businesses will fail
Practical Difficulties for Business in International Trade	• Language	• Printing instructions • Negotiating prices	• Costs of accurate translation • Need to hire language consultant

Topic	Key Features	Detail	Further Information
Practical Difficulties for Business in International Trade *cont.*	• Currency	• Costs of changing currency	• Exchange rates change. Costs difficult to anticipate
	• Transport	• Long distances involved add to costs	• May need specialist lorries, etc.
Protectionism	• Tariffs	• Tax on imports	• Increases price of imports • Makes home products seem cheaper
	• Quotas	• Restriction on number of imports	• Often a % of home market
	• Technical	• Laws on how goods are made	• E.g. On pollution levels from vehicles
Problems of Protectionism	• Retaliation	• Other countries restrict your exports	• All countries suffer with lack of trade
	• Price rises	• Foreign goods cost more with tariffs	• Inflation increase in home country
	• Legal problems	• Actions taken may be illegal	• E.g. French ban on British beef
	• May support inefficiency	• Older inefficient industries survive with protection	• Keeps costs high in home country
Exchange Rates	• Stable exchange rate	• Exchange rates remain the same	• E.g. £1= €1.5 stays the same
	• Rising value of £	• Importers benefit • Exporters have problems	• E.g. £1= €1.5 changes to £1= €1.6
	• Falling value of £	• Importers have problems • Exporters benefit	• E.g. £1= €1.5 changes to £1= €1.4
European Union (EU)	• 15 members at present (2003) • Started in 1957	• Issues many directives which affect business	• E.g. Cooling off period with doorstop sales
	• Aim to cooperate more closely	• E.g. European Central Bank	• Controls economic policy of Euro zone
Benefits of EU Membership for Business	• Enlarged market	• More opportunity for sales and cost savings	
		• 10 more countries to join in 2004	• Mainly from Eastern Europe

Topic	Key Features	Detail	Further Information
Benefits of EU Membership for Business *cont*.	• Single market	• Started 1 September 1993	• Easier trade within EU
	• Common standards of products	• Saves making different goods for different countries	• E.g. Electrical standards for home appliances
	• Grants and subsidies	• Helps businesses in poorer areas	• E.g. Restructuring after coal and steel closures
Problems of EU Membership for Business	• Enlarged market	• More competition may mean job losses	
	• Social Chapter	• Increase costs for some business	• E.g. Minimum wage
	• Environmental standards	• More costs to meet pollution controls, etc.	• Water industry has been affected
Single European Currency	• 12 of 15 members of EU use the Euro (2003) • Use started in January 2002	• UK yet to decide	• Vote some time in the future
Advantages of Joining Single Currency	• Cost savings	• No costs of changing currency within Euro zone	• Less costs = more profit opportunity
	• Stable exchange rate	• Enables businesses to plan ahead with more certainty	
Problems of Joining Single Currency	• Adds to costs	• Cost of changing tills, etc.	
	• Loss of the £	• Britain will lose the £ as a currency	• Seen by some as a loss of control over economy
	• Difficult to reverse	• Once decision is made, very difficult to change	• Must be certain of joining

The Location of Business

Topic	Key Features	Detail	Further Information
Why Important to Business	• May be the difference between success and failure	• Once started, difficult and expensive to move again	• Choice must be carefully made
Raw Materials	• Reduce cost of expensive transport of heavy goods	• Steel works near iron ore supplies • Oil refineries on the coast	• E.g. Sheffield and South Wales steelworks • E.g. Milford Haven oil refineries
Transport	• The need to have quick deliveries in and out. Cuts costs	• Includes road, rail, air, and coastal locations • Motorway locations near junctions for easy access	• Important in delivery business • Lorries need main road location for delivery
Labour	• Important for labour intensive business	• Can mean looking worldwide for cheapest location	• E.g. Trainers made in Far East • Call centres now located worldwide
Costs	• Cost of land important	• E.g. Supermarkets need large areas of flat land, cost is vital	• Land cheaper in northern England • Edge of cities cheaper than centre
Government Aid	• Incentives for location in certain areas	• High unemployment areas targeted	• Some areas often unattractive without incentives
Near to Market	• Cuts cost of transport to customers	• Affects many businesses • Some goods need to be fresh	• E.g. Most shops, bakeries
Traditions	• Once established, difficult to move	• Location name may help product • Skills in area for future workers	• Sheffield steel an example
Enterprise Zones	• Small areas giving advantages to business	• Simplified planning • Tax allowances • No Business Rates for 10 years • Help with training • Infrastructure improvements	• Can greatly reduce business costs • May lead to poor location being chosen if costs the only consideration
Assisted Areas	• Larger areas receiving aid	• Rural areas benefit • Former coal and steel areas targeted	• Receive less assistance than Enterprise Zones

Topic	Key Features	Detail	Further Information
Regional Development Agencies	• Co-ordinate investment	• Local skills improved • Advice on aid applications • Improvements to local environment • Help economic regeneration	• Workers may need training in new skills • Great help to smaller business with advice

Types of Market

Topic	Key Features	Detail	Further Information
Competition	• Many buyers and sellers of products and services	• Businesses usually small • No one business influences others • Great choice for consumer	• Easy to set up in business • Businesses compete on price and service • E.g. Small 'corner' shops
Oligopoly	• A few firms control most sales	• Usually much larger businesses • Often 'agree' on prices • Actions of one followed by others	• E.g. Petrol companies • Compete on promotions and location
Monopoly	• One producer controls at least 25% of sales	• Business may produce one product • Little real competition • Consumer has little choice • However, can benefit consumer	• Prices may be higher with less choice • Prices could be lower with economies of scale
Government and Competition	• The Law	• European Union directives • Price fixing illegal • Forcing prices up by selling less is illegal	
	• Office of Fair Trading	• Tries to encourage competition	
	• Watchdogs	• Control the former Public Utilities e.g. Electricity	• Price and service levels monitored
	• Competition Commission	• Checks if mergers are in the public interest	• Checks on actions of possible monopolies

PUTTING IT IN CONTEXT

Doulwedge plc is a pottery business, specialising in high quality pottery and china. For many years it has *exported* products throughout the world, realising that a *larger market* will not only *spread the risks* of the business, but also give the opportunity of *economies of large scale production*. Whilst cutting *unit costs* for the business, there was the possibility of *increasing profit*.

In recent years, *international trade* has meant that *cheaper imports* have taken some of the trade from Doulwedge plc. There have been some *job losses* at their main factory in Oldcastle as a result of this *competition*. Because Doulwedge plc is not an inefficient business, they feel they have a good future. The management see no need for *tariffs* or *quotas* to *restrict the imports* as this would possibly mean *retaliation* from the countries to which Doulwedge plc exported.

The business is hoping to start exporting to new countries, but understands that there will be *extra costs* in doing this, notably *new language brochures* and the *extra costs of transport*. The possible expansion of the *European Union* will certainly be a new *target market* for the company.

UK membership of the *EU* influenced the introduction of the *minimum wage* into the country. This had less effect on Doulwedge plc than other local businesses. They already paid their workers above the *minimum level* and so had no concern about *rising costs* which were affecting some of their competitors.

Recent rises in the *value of the £* against other currencies have meant *exporting* is proving more difficult for the business. These *exchange rate changes* have meant that *exports have become dearer* in countries to which Doulwedge plc sells. The company would like to see Britain joining the *Single European Currency* (Euro) as this would help *stabilise exchange rates* and *make future planning clearer*.

The main factory site was *located* in Oldcastle nearly 200 years ago because the necessary *raw material* (clay) was found nearby. Over the years *local labour* developed the necessary high levels of skills required for the business. The local clay has now all but run out, but the *location* has not been moved as the local pottery *tradition* has meant that the 'Made in Oldcastle' helps sell the pottery and it would be *costly to move* and retrain a new workforce elsewhere.

Possible future expansion of the business to include a craft shop and tour centre for schools may well attract *Government support*, as Oldcastle is in an *Assisted Area* due to the *high levels of employment* in the local area.

Other possibilities in the future would be the *merger* of Doulwedge plc and Gildro plc, though this would create a *monopoly*, as the enlarged business would control more than *25% of the pottery market*. Such a move would mean that there would be an investigation by the *Competition Commission* in order to see if the merger was in the *interests of the consumer*.

ACTIVITIES

ACTIVITY ONE

For each of the following businesses, explain the factors that would be considered in choosing a suitable location for the business:

- A factory making trainers.
- A mail order delivery centre.
- A hypermarket.
- A fish and chip shop.
- A research laboratory concentrating on the development of new drugs.
- A factory which freezes fresh vegetables.

ACTIVITY TWO

When the exchange rate of the £ changes, there is an effect on both importers and exporters. Complete the following flow consequence diagram to explain the results of the changes. The first has been started for you.

Draw similar consequence diagrams for b) and c):

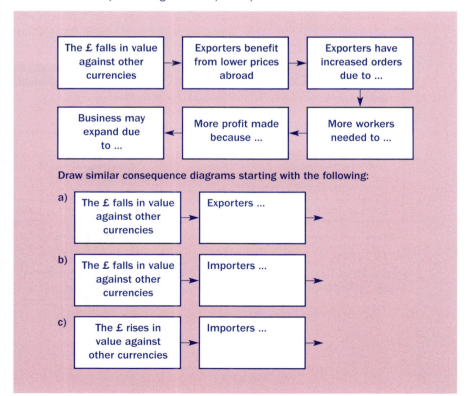

ACTIVITY THREE

Many industries in Britain have changed due to international trade and competition.

a) Look around your house and find at least 10 products, such as clothing, electrical goods, furniture, etc. Look where each of the products was made

b) Draw a bar graph to show your results. Use three categories for your graph, made in the UK, made in Europe, made in the rest of the world. Comment on the findings shown in the graph.

c) Choose any three products that are made *outside* the UK. Explain why these are imported and then bought in the UK, rather than being home produced.

Many goods we now buy are imported

ACTIVITY FOUR

Complete the following chart to explain the problems and benefits of membership of the European Union. Make your chart large enough for detailed explanations. Some features may be in both benefits and problem columns; others will only be in one.

Feature	Benefit because...	Problem because...
Enlarged market		
Single market		
Social Charter		
Environmental standards		
Common standards for products		
Grants and subsidies		

ACTIVITY FIVE

In October 2002 Granada Television and Carlton Television announced they would like to merge. Before this could happen, the Competition Commission would have to agree.

ACTIVITIES *cont.*

a) What does the Competition Commission do?
b) Why should the Competition Commission be involved in this merger of two television companies?
c) With the help of your teacher, try and find other mergers that are taking place now. Explain why or why not the Competition Commission is involved in the merger.

 QUESTION TYPES TO EXPECT

AQA 'A' questions may ask you to give the meaning and examples of terms such as:

- *Tariffs*
- *Quotas*
- *Exchange rates*
- *Social Charter*
- *European Union*
- *Single European Currency*
- *Importers and Exporters*
- *Monopoly*
- *Oligopoly*
- *Competition*
- *Assisted Areas*
- *Enterprise Zones*
- *Competition Commission*
- *'Watchdogs'*
- *Office of Fair Trading*

There are many practical problems in international trade

More difficult questions that you may be asked in AQA specification 'A' or specification 'B':

- *Identify and explain the benefits and problems caused by international trade.*
- *Explain the effects of cheaper imported goods on particular industries in the UK.*
- *Evaluate the merits of protectionism in international trade.*
- *Evaluate the benefits and problems caused by the UK's membership of the European Union.*
- *Calculate the effects of a change in the value of the £ to both importers and exporters.*
- *Interpret and evaluate numerical data relating to exchange rate changes.*

The Changing Business Environment

- *Identify and explain the problems and benefits of joining the Single European Currency.*
- *Analyse the reasons why businesses locate in particular areas.*
- *Explain the role of government in business location decisions.*
- *Identify and explain the differences between different types of market.*
- *Explain how and why the UK government takes an interest in large business mergers and takeovers.*
- *Explain the possible advantages and disadvantages of competitive markets to the consumer.*
- *Explain the possible advantages and disadvantages of monopolies to the consumer.*

Some examples of these types of questions and student answers are given in the following section. Look carefully at what the question is asking you to do; how the student has answered the question; what the examiner thinks of the answer.

THE CHANGING BUSINESS ENVIRONMENT: SPECIMEN QUESTIONS

Question one (a) Common Question b) Higher Tier)
Printit Ltd export calendars and diaries to different countries throughout the world.

a) Explain **two** possible benefits to Printit Ltd of exporting to different countries. **(4)**
b) Explain how the following might affect Printit Ltd:
   i) Other countries putting tariffs on imports.
   ii) Other countries putting quotas on imports. **(6)**

Student Answer

a)   *If Printit Ltd do export to different countries they are taking a market share in different markets besides their own, this can give them support in harder times if their own market economy is not doing so well. Also they can hire people to work in different countries, if they can find the suitable skilled workers – they would need to have language qualifications, the job would be made more desirable as it would be in a different country.*

b) *If a country that Printit exports to puts a tariff on their imports this would cause the Printit product to be more expensive than the native products and hence causing Printit's profit from that country to fall as people would be buying the cheaper native goods.*

If a country did put a quota on imports it would limit the amount Printit could sell in that country and due to that Printit's profits would be in turn limited.

Mark

What the Examiner Says

a) Mark has correctly identified one benefit, that of spreading risk. If the economy of one country is in decline, then exports sales in other countries would indeed help the business. In the second example there seems to be some confusion as the answer seems to suggest workers producing the goods in different countries. This has no real connection with the question which asks for the benefits of exporting to different countries.

A further example which outlined the benefits from increased production and so reduction of costs (economies of scale) would have gained full marks.

Marks awarded – 2 out of 4

b) Mark has correctly identified the fact that an introduction of tariffs will increase the price of imports, which will mean (possibly) lower profits as consumers will switch to the lower priced 'native' products. In fact consumers may well buy the imports at a higher price if home products are inferior. This however is not certain.

Quotas will mean a lowering of the amount of goods Printit Ltd will be able to export. There is once again the potential for lower profits, as identified by Mark, though this is not developed. Printit Ltd might, in fact, be able to put up the price of their products if there is sufficient demand.

Marks awarded – 5 out of 6

Question two (Higher Tier)

JMY Ltd makes light fittings which are exported to the European Union.

a) Explain the possible problems of European Union membership to a business such as JMY Ltd. The market for light fittings is very competitive. **(6)**

b) The value of the Euro to the £ has increased from £1 = €1.5, to £1 = €1.7. Explain how this change in value of the Euro might affect JMY Ltd. **(6)**

Student Answer

a)   There is a lot of competition for light fittings, which means that JMY Ltd
       must be very careful about increasing their prices, otherwise this will
       mean that they lose customers. As Britain is in the EU, other businesses
abroad can export their goods easily to Britain without any restrictions. This will mean
that JMY has even more competition and may lose business. The EU introduce laws and
directives which affect businesses. This might affect the way they work and increase
costs, such as the minimum wage, and the working time directive, which puts a limit on
the hours an employee should work.

b) If the price of the pound has increased abroad then it would cause the price of all JMY's
    products that are exported to different countries who have the Euro to increase. This would
    cause the profits in that country, which is importing the products to drop as JMY's product,
    will be more expensive than its competitors. For instance if the product was priced at €3 a
    fall in the value of the Euro would increase the price of the same product to €3.4.

Katy

What the Examiner Says

a) The answer given by Katy centres upon two ideas; competition
    and laws. Both these ideas are well developed with examples
    given as to how they impact upon the business. The examples of
    the minimum wage and working time directive are well chosen.

Marks awarded – 6 out of 6

b) Katy has correctly identified that this change in value of the £
    against the Euro will affect *all* the countries which are in the Euro
    zone. It is also correct to say that the price of the product will
    increase in the Euro zone, even giving a correct mathematical
    example. The fall in profits of the country importing the goods is
    a little confusing and not fully linked to an effect on Printit Ltd.

    Katy could have explored the connection between a rise in the
    cost of the light fittings abroad and a fall in demand which in turn
    would have meant fewer orders. This may then have led to some
    workers being laid off, or new markets having to be found outside
    the Euro zone which are not affected by currency changes etc.

Marks awarded – 3 out of 6

Question Three (Common Question)

Oscar Ltd supply parts for computers. They promise next day delivery on parts which are ordered before 5pm. The management at Oscar Ltd is looking for a new location for the parts warehouse. Explain how the following might affect the decision on where to locate the new warehouse.

a) Government aid
b) Transport links to the warehouse **(6)**

Student Answer

a)   *Oscar Ltd locate their warehouse in a redevelopment area then it is possible to receive government aid, this is offered to entice businesses to set up their business here and make jobs for the local residents. This will influence Oscar Ltd because they will have to take into account the opportunity of receiving aid for just setting up their warehouse in a certain area.*

b) *As Oscar Ltd promise next day delivery, they must make sure they are next to transport links that can make this possible. The best place to locate would be next to a busy motorway junction, where more than two motorways meet. This will mean that lorries can get in and out to deliver the parts quickly and Oscar Ltd can keep their promise. If this was next to a large city it would be even better as this is where the customers will be for the computer parts. This would help cut time for delivery (and costs) even more.*

Suzanne

What the Examiner Says

a) Suzanne has recognised that governments 'entice' businesses to particular areas by giving aid, which will be to the benefit of the business itself and local residents. This will indeed be considered by the business, though the answer could have been more precise with an example such as relief from Business Rates and how this will reduce the costs of the business.

b) This is a much better answer with a clear link being made to the benefits of good transport links (motorway junction, just outside large cities) for a business which must deliver (and collect for delivery) items the next day. The link between time and costs is well made.

Marks awarded – 5 (2 + 3) out of 6

Question Four (Higher Tier)

Evaluate the considerations a foreign car manufacturer such as Nissan and Toyota might make in deciding on a location for a new car production centre. **(8)**

Student Answer

If either Nissan or Toyota did decide to place a new car plant in the UK then there would be obvious benefits such as government aid offered to them to attract them to certain parts of the country where there is high unemployment. As they would need large amounts of both skilled and unskilled workers then the government would offer them a great deal of aid to set up their plant in a certain area so that the government can say they have reduced unemployment in that area due to the new car plant offering large amounts of employment.

Also they, too, would have to think about transporting their cars across the country to their many showrooms so that the cars can be sold to the public. This would influence them because they wouldn't want to set up their car plant in an area that didn't have good transportation links to the rest of the country.

Both these factors contribute to the decision-making of where to set up a car plant. It is the board of directors of both companies jobs to make a compromise between the two, if one should arise that is. For instance it would be useless setting up a car plant in the middle of nowhere just so that the company can receive government aid.

Conrad

What the Examiner Says

The command word in this question is 'evaluate'. This means that a judgement must be made as to the factors that have the *greatest* influence *in this particular case*.

Conrad has judged correctly that this particular business will be of considerable size, requiring large amounts of skilled and unskilled labour, which would itself attract government aid if located in certain areas. This particular business would also require the stated transport links to transport the finished goods to market.

Whilst this identification of the factors affecting location is good (the sheer size of the required site could have been included) the *evaluation* of the factors is rather lacking. A general statement is made that the company should not consider a place just because it receives aid, but this is not developed. Conrad should have considered importance the different factors he identified and made a judgement as to which are the more important, giving reasons for that decision.

This answer is at the lower part of Level 2 (5–8 marks). Further evaluation is necessary, with reasons, to move further into this Level.

3

PART THREE

CASE STUDY

The Case Study for each Specification is different. The Case Study for AQA Specification A is pre-released. There are two types of Case Study for AQA Specification B; one is for paper 1, the other is for the examination paper that can be taken as an alternative to coursework. Below is some general advice on dealing with Case Studies and some specific advice for each option.

GENERAL ADVICE

A Case Study will be a study of a single business – plus possibly its dealings with its stakeholders and other businesses. It will have been written to highlight a specific part of a business or to just give you general information on a business. It will have, like a story, a setting, characters and events taking place. Case Studies are also designed to provide a context in which various terms, methods and ideas can be investigated. For example, the way that a small business may raise finance will be different to that of a large public company; the options, in terms of advertising and marketing for a small business will be different to those available for a larger one and so on. Much of the teaching in your course will have taken place through the use of Case Studies, so you should be familiar with them. Text books such as the *AQA Business Studies for Specification A* and the *AQA GCSE Business Studies B (2nd Edition)* have numerous Case Studies on which you can practise.

To get the best out of a Case Study:

- Read the Case Study thoroughly first – you can do this quite quickly, in order to gain a general picture of what is going on
- Read it a second time and mark up anything that you don't immediately understand
- Read it a third time, this time thoroughly, and highlight important words and phrases, such as terms and methods that have been used
- Even in an examination, it is worth spending this time on reading, so that you are familiar with the context. There is no need to rush to start straight away, in fact, some examination papers advise or insist on a certain period of reading time.

SPECIFICATION A – CASE STUDY AND SAMPLE QUESTIONS

The Specification A Case Study is pre-released. In other words, you will have chance to read and study it before the examination. It will arrive in your school or college about three months before the examination. You should not contact the company that is used, but there is nothing to stop you gaining a wider knowledge by collecting literature on the business or by visiting its website. The extra information you gain will give you a better idea about the business but you must remember that everything you will need to answer the questions on the examination paper will be contained in the Case Study. Case Studies are based on real businesses and have included Ford Motors, McDonald's, Tesco and British Airways. The specimen paper provided by the board uses McDonald's and looks at the following areas:

- Ownership
- Growth
- Franchising
- Business location
- Stakeholders
- External influences and issues
- Organisational structures
- Motivation
- Employee benefits
- Marketing
- Measuring financial performance.

Once you have received, read and marked up the Case Study, you then have time to make sure that you understand all the terms and methods contained in it. To do this you should use your text book to:

- get a clear definition of each term and write it up in language that you understand
- make sure that you know how (and why) each method is used.

Keep coming back to the Case Study and use it for your revision. You can do exercises on your own or with other students to sharpen your understanding. Also try to guess what questions the examiner might be going to ask. Remember, the Case Study will have been written a year to eighteen months before you receive it, so anything that has happened in the last year is unlikely to be included. But what about at the time it was written? You could look in newspaper archive sites on the internet for any major issues that were happening at the time. Always remember, though, the information that you need will all be contained in the Case Study.

CASE STUDY EXAMPLE

The Case Study material is on The Body Shop. There are forty words and phrases that you need to know and be able to define (and use); these have been highlighted for you but it would be up to you to find them yourself. Start by making sure that you have a clear definition and understanding of all of these. The numbers in the case study refer to places where you could make notes to guess at possible questions that could be asked. Make a numbered list and fill in the sort of questions which you think might be asked, then check it against the examiner's own comments (on page 134).

THE BODY SHOP

The Body Shop has built itself an international reputation as an organisation that produces a range of products that are, as far as possible, environmentally friendly. It stocks a variety of products which have not been tested on animals and which, in the way that they are produced and sold, cause as little damage to the environment as possible.

The information below is taken from the Body Shop website and from the 2002 Annual Report and Accounts of Body Shop International plc.

*The Body Shop International **plc** is a values driven, high quality skin and body care **retailer** operating in 50 countries with over 1,900 outlets spanning 25 languages and 12 time zones **[see note 1]**. Famous for creating a **niche market** sector for naturally inspired skin and hair care products, The Body Shop introduced a generation of **consumers** to the benefits of a wide range of best sellers from Vitamin E Moisture Cream to the Tea Tree Oil range and Banana Shampoo.*

*It is estimated that The Body Shop sells a **product** every 0.4 seconds with over 77 million customers transactions through stores worldwide, with customers sampling the current range of over 600 products and more than 400 accessories **[see note 1]**. The Body Shop has always believed that business is primarily about human relationships. We believe that the more we listen to our **stakeholders** and involve them in decision making, the better our business will run **[see note 2]**.*

*In 1999 The Body Shop **brand** was voted the second most trusted brand in the UK by the **Consumers Association** [see note 3]. According to the 1997 Interbrand survey criteria, the company was named 28th top brand in the world, second in the retail sector. In a 1998 report, a survey of international chief executives in The Financial Times ranked The Body Shop the 27th most respected company in the world.*

THE BODY SHOP *MISSION STATEMENT*

The Body Shop International plc – a company with a difference

*To dedicate our business to the pursuit of **social and environmental change** [see note 4].*

THE BODY SHOP

*To creatively balance the financial and human needs of our stakeholders: employees, customers, **franchisees**, suppliers and shareholders [see note 4].*

*To courageously ensure that our business is **ecologically sustainable**: meeting the needs of the present without compromising the future.*

To meaningfully contribute to local, national and international communities in which we trade, by adopting a code of conduct which ensures care, honesty, fairness and respect.

To passionately campaign for the protection of the environment, human and civil rights, and against animal testing within the cosmetics and toiletries industry.

To tirelessly work to narrow the gap between principle and practice, whilst making fun, passion and care part of our daily lives

HISTORY

*The Body Shop rapidly evolved from one small shop in Brighton, opened by Anita Roddick, on the south coast of England, with only around 25 hand-mixed products on sale, to a worldwide network of shops. **Franchising** allowed for rapid growth and international expansion as hundreds of **entrepreneurs** worldwide bought into Anita's vision [see note 5].*

The Company's campaigns against human rights abuses, in favour of animal and environmental protection and its commitment to challenge the stereotypes of beauty perpetuated by the cosmetics industry, have won the support of generations of consumers. The company continues to lead the way for businesses to use their voice for social and environmental change.

COMPANY LANDMARKS

The 1970s

26th March 1976 – The Body Shop opens for business and brings the benefits of previously unheard of natural ingredients to the high street – aloe vera, jojoba oil, rhassoul mud, cocoa butter – and many more.

1978

*A kiosk in Brussels becomes the first overseas **franchise** in 1978 [see note 6].*

The 1980s

1982

New shops opening at a rate of two per month.

1985

*In 1985, in its first year as a **public company**, The Body Shop sponsored posters for Greenpeace. A year later, it created an Environmental Projects Department of its own.*

1986

The first Community Trade product for The Body Shop was a footsie roller, produced in 1986 by a supplier in southern India. This trade in footsie rollers has evolved into the current trade with Teddy Exports in India.

The Body Shop sets up its own in-house Environmental department.

The Body Shop ran its first major campaign in alliance with Greenpeace; Save the Whale.

1989

Our 'Stop The Burning' campaign, called for the Brazilian Government to bring a halt to the mass burning of the tropical rainforests. One million customers signed the petition that Anita Roddick presented to the Brazilian embassy.

The 1990s

1990

In 1990, just one year after launching in the USA, there were 2,500 applications for a franchise. **Demand** for The Body Shop product is vast, driving a geographical expansion that saw the company trading in 39 countries only fourteen years after the first shop opened.

The establishment of The Body Shop Foundation in 1990, a **charity** which funds human rights and environmental protection groups [**see note 7**].

1991

The Big Issue homeless paper which started as a project of The Body Shop Foundation was launched in 1991.

1992

The introduction of The Body Shop Tour at the UK Head Office for the general public in 1992.

1993

In 1993 the Company launched an international campaign to raise awareness of the plight of the Ogoni people and their leader Ken Saro-Wiwa, persecuted for protesting against Shell and the Nigerian dictatorship over exploitation in their homeland.

1994

The Body Shop At Home, the **direct-selling** arm, was launched in the UK in 1994, Canada in 1995 and Australia in 1997 [**see note 8**]. Today in the UK alone, there are over 3000 consultants who introduced 940,484 customers to The Body Shop and its product at 103,762 parties in 2000/2001. Spring 2001 sees the launch of The Body Shop At Home in Ireland and the USA later in the year.

The Body Shop continues to increase its environmental practices [**see note 9**]. In 2001, The Body Shop UK region and service centre head offices switched to Ecotricity providing them

with *energy from renewable sources*. In addition, 127 of The Body Shop UK stores have now converted to **green electricity** with the rest of the stores due to follow suit.

1995

The New Academy of Business, an initiative of Anita Roddick, was established in 1995. The innovative **management** degree, addressing social, environmental and ethical issues, is run at The University of Bath.

1996

Campaign successes including the Against Animal Testing campaign, which led to the largest ever petition (with four million signatures) being delivered to the **European Commission** in 1996 *[see note 9]*. The campaign led to a UK-wide ban on animal testing on cosmetic products and ingredients in November 1998.

1997

In 1997, The Body Shop was the first international cosmetics company to sign up to the Humane Cosmetics Standard supported by leading animal protection groups.

The Body Shop Values Reports in 1995 and 1997 were recognised by United Nations Environmental Programme and SustainAbility, as trailblazing, and ranked highest in their review of International Corporate Environmental Reports.

In 1997, The Body Shop celebrated its 21st birthday with the launch of a new **flagship store** design which won the prestigious Retail Week Store Design of the Year Award.

1998

To celebrate the 50th Anniversary of the Universal Declaration of Human Rights in 1998, The Body Shop launched a joint worldwide campaign with Amnesty International to highlight the plight of human rights defenders around the world, encouraging customers to 'Make their Mark' for human rights. Three million people signed up to the campaign.

The Body Shop Foundation part-funded the launch of The Big Issue in Los Angeles in early 1998.

1999

A **loyalty scheme** for customers was introduced to the UK in the autumn of 1999 *[see note 10]*. It provides incentives to customers, including the option to donate reward money to selected campaign organisations, including World Society for the Protection of Animals and the Missing Persons Helpline.

In 1999, The Body Shop created four new business units in the UK, Europe, the Americas and Asia, shifting its **operational and management structure** out to the regions. The change was implemented to focus more of our resources closer to the markets and to create a more flexible and efficient operating structure across the Group. It is believed that this **decentralised structure** will significantly enhance The Company's ability to deliver a tailored offer to our customers faster and more efficiently *[see note 11]*.

The 2000s

2000

In February 2000, the Company completed the sale of its Littlehampton **manufacturing** business to Creative Outsourcing Solutions International Ltd (COSi).

The Body Shop Human Rights Award was launched to **media**, non-governmental organisations and the public in June 2000. The Award has been set up to seek out and recognise individuals and grassroots organisations focusing on social, economic and cultural rights. Every two years, The Body Shop Human Rights Award will acknowledge community based projects around the globe, giving them not only recognition, but also practical and financial help. The theme for the 2000 Award was child labour and its role in denying children, particularly girls, a basic education.

In 2000/2001, The Body Shop purchased over £5 million worth of natural ingredients and accessory items through the Community Trade Programme including nearly 400 tonnes of natural ingredients.

2001

The Body Shop branches into South Africa. In June 2001, The Body Shop agreed to appoint a major South African retailer, New Clicks Holdings, as The Body Shop direct franchisee in South Africa. New Clicks has a strong commitment to **corporate social responsibility** through its New Clicks Foundation. The first The Body Shop stores will open in Cape Town and Johannesburg in October 2001.

March 26th 2001 Happy Birthday! The Body Shop celebrates 25 years of 'business as unusual.' Celebrating 25 years of a great experiment – an experiment which proved it is possible to build a huge global enterprise and still challenge, campaign, trade honourably, give back to the community and have a good time while doing it.

The Journey Continues

Activism has been part of the DNA of The Body Shop. The last 25 years have been a testament to an extraordinary partnership with millions of men, women and children all over the globe. And what about the next 25 years? The unique blend of product, passion and partnership that characterises the story of The Body Shop will continue to evolve. It is a shared vision. So the great experiment goes on.

A SELECTION OF FIGURES

[see note 12]

UK & Republic of Ireland

	2002	2001
Shops at year end	325	304
Shop openings (net)	10	29
Company-owned stores	181	159

THE BODY SHOP

	£m	£m	Change
Retail sales	181.3	180	+ 0.7%
Turnover	149.4	147.9	+ 1%
Operating **profit**	20.5	27.4	– 25%

The Body Shop, being international in make-up, has to cope with changes in the value of foreign currencies, most importantly, the **exchange rates** for the US dollar and the European Euro.

	Year end 2002	Year end 2001
US$	1.42	1.47
Euro	1.64	1.58

EMPLOYEES AND EMPLOYEE INVOLVEMENT

[see note 13]

The Body Shop aims to nurture a committed and **motivated** employee group with improving skills and knowledge. The Company's policy is for **training**, career development and **promotion opportunities** to be available to all employees. **Applications for employment by disabled people** are given full and fair consideration for all vacancies, taking into account their particular skills and abilities. If any employee becomes disabled while working for the Company, every effort is made to retain them. One of the formal ways in which the Company consults employees in the UK and Europe is via a **Consultation** and Representation Committee, consisting of employee-elected representatives. In addition, it uses **focus groups** and **surveys** to elicit views from employees on issues affecting their employment relationship with the Company. The Company has also offered a successful advocacy service since 1997, consisting of a group of employees who are trained to assist other employees with difficulties, such as **grievance and disciplinary situations**.

Profit and Loss Account for the 52 weeks ended 2 March 2002 (simplified)

[see note 14]

	2002 £m	2001 £m
Turnover	377.7	374.1
Cost of sales	(148.1)	(149.0)
Gross profit	229.6	225.1
Operating expenses	(201.7)	(195.7)
Net profit	27.9	29.4

Reproduced with the kind permission of the copyright holder The Body Shop International plc.

Forty terms and concepts highlighted to learn.

1. applications for employment by disabled people
2. brand
3. charity
4. consultation
5. consumers
6. Consumers Association
7. corporate social responsibility
8. decentralised structure
9. demand
10. direct-selling
11. ecologically sustainable
12. energy from renewable sources
13. entrepreneurs
14. European Commission
15. exchange rates
16. flagship store
17. focus groups
18. franchise
19. franchisees
20. franchising
21. green electricity
22. grievance and disciplinary situations
23. loyalty scheme
24. manufacturing
25. media
26. mission statement
27. motivated
28. niche market
29. operational and management structure
30. plc
31. profit
32. Profit and Loss Account
33. promotion opportunities
34. public company
35. retailer
36. social and environmental change
37. stakeholders
38. surveys
39. training
40. turnover

Examiner's thoughts on possible questions

1. Possible questions on business ownership – What are the features of a plc? Possible question on chain of production – consumers and retailers are mentioned. Possible question on types of market – niche vs mass for example.

2. Possible question on stakeholders – What are they? Why are they important?

3. Question on branding and its importance to a business.

4. Several possibilities. The idea of the Body Shop being concerned with social and environmental issues and issues such as sustainability is bound to be used somewhere, as is a question on franchising. The question on stakeholders could be here, as they are listed. More likely, here, is a question on the aims and objectives of businesses, as stated in documents like mission statements.

5. What are entrepreneurs? Why are they important – and to whom?

6. As this is about growth, it is likely that the franchising question will come here. It will, however, draw from other parts of the Case Study.

7. A possible question on demand, and the factors that affect demand. A possible question on the differences between a charity as a business organisation and a public company.

8. What is direct selling? What are its advantages and disadvantages?

9. What is the European Commission? What is its role in the EU?

10. How does a loyalty scheme operate, what is its purpose? How could a loyalty scheme fit in with other elements of the marketing mix (such as branding, product life cycle, direct selling as a means of distribution...)?

11. Questions on organisational structure. Why should a decentralised structure be better? What is the alternative? What are the good and bad features of different organisational structures? There could also be questions here on management styles.

12. Possible questions on an interpretation of the figures, looking, in particular, at growth and profitability.

13. Questions based on the human resources section of the content. There could be questions on motivation, employee involvement, training issues, grievance procedures, consultation and legislation (such as the Disability Discrimination Act). There could also be a question relating to how opinions are sought i.e. on focus groups and surveys, this could then be linked to the use of these in market research.

14. Possible questions on profitability and on some financial ratios.

Remember that you can always refer to other parts of the Case Study to help you to answer a question.

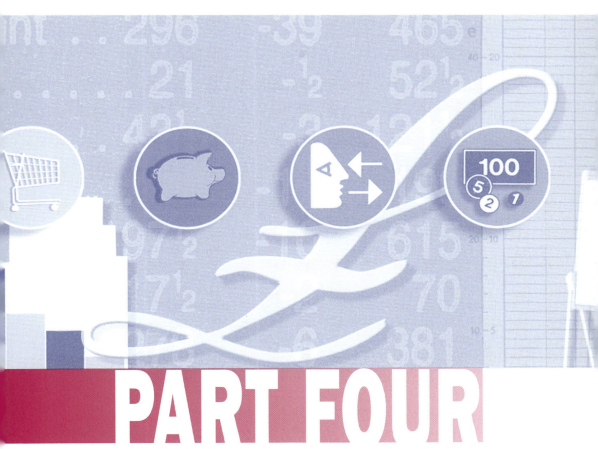

4

PART FOUR

SAMPLE QUESTIONS FOR AQA 'A'

Candidates are always allowed to either draw examples from the Case Study or from their own knowledge of Business Studies. You will see from the questions which businesses have been used for the Case Studies. Questions have been re-phrased or re-written, where necessary, so that the information from the Case Study can be bypassed. The 2001 questions are taken from the Specimen Examination Material produced by the examination board. Most questions which require Candidates to merely define terms have also been left out.

The External Environment of Business

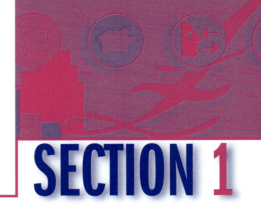

SECTION 1

Foundation

1999

1. Explain how information technology might help a firm, such as a hotel, to run its business. Use examples to illustrate your answer. **(6 marks)**

2000

2. Many businesses now use the internet to sell their products.
    a) State three difficulties that might be experienced with this method of selling. **(3 marks)**
    b) Briefly explain how using Information and Communication Technology (ICT) may help a business to run more efficiently. **(3 marks)**

2001

3. McDonald's is planning to open a new restaurant in a small town called Benson.

Figure 1 Opening a new restaurant

McDonald's is always looking for new sites to expand its business. Benson is among the sites in which it is interested.

Location of Benson

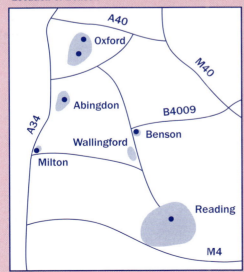

Benson has a population of about 4000, which includes the population of the nearby RAF base. Many people who live in Benson commute to work in nearby towns, such as Oxford. Public transport links between Benson and Oxford and Wallingford are good. The region has a lower than average level of unemployment. Most of the houses in Benson are owner-occupied and, like most of Oxfordshire, house prices tend to be much higher than the national average. However, the village of Benson accommodates a good social mix of people. Benson is a popular location for families and there is a thriving primary school in the village.

The site that has been identified for the McDonald's restaurant lies on a roundabout on the A4074, just outside the village. There is already a petrol station and a car showroom there.

---

a) If McDonald's opens a restaurant in Benson, discuss how this could affect other businesses nearby. **(8 marks)**

4. Use the information supplied in the Case Study to answer the questions below.

You have been asked by McDonald's to produce a report on whether the company should open one of its restaurants in Benson.

When writing your report you should remember to:
- write in the correct style for a report
- examine the advantages of Benson as a possible site
- consider any problems McDonald's might have if Benson was chosen
- weigh up the arguments for and against using Benson
- give a recommendation as to whether a restaurant should be opened in Benson.

(14 marks)

Higher

2001

5. Look at Figure 1 on page 137.

The Case Study looks at the possibility of McDonald's opening a new restaurant in Benson.
a) Giving two reasons, consider why McDonald's believes that Benson is a suitable location for one of its restaurants. **(4 marks)**
b) If McDonald's opens a restaurant in Benson, consider how this could affect other businesses nearby. **(6 marks)**

6. a) Like other fast-food businesses, McDonald's has restaurants in many different countries around the world. Give two possible reasons why businesses decide to open restaurants in other countries. **(2 marks)**
b) What problems might a business like McDonald's have selling its products in a foreign country? **(4 marks)**

7. Pressure groups have criticised McDonald's and other fast food companies for the impact they have on the environment.
a) Give two examples of how fast food companies can affect the environment.
b) Describe two strategies fast food chains like McDonald's may follow to improve their public image on environmental issues. **(4 marks)**

Business Structure, Organisation and Control

SECTION 2

Foundation

1989

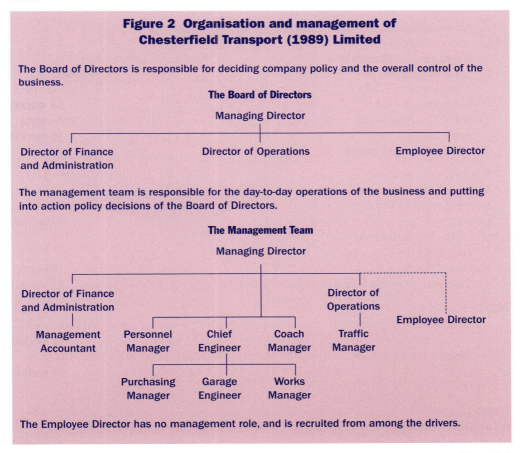

Figure 2 Organisation and management of Chesterfield Transport (1989) Limited

The Board of Directors is responsible for deciding company policy and the overall control of the business.

The Board of Directors

Managing Director

Director of Finance and Administration   Director of Operations   Employee Director

The management team is responsible for the day-to-day operations of the business and putting into action policy decisions of the Board of Directors.

The Management Team

Managing Director

Director of Finance and Administration   Director of Operations   Employee Director

Management Accountant   Personnel Manager   Chief Engineer   Coach Manager   Traffic Manager

Purchasing Manager   Garage Engineer   Works Manager

The Employee Director has no management role, and is recruited from among the drivers.

1. a) Explain the benefits of organising Chesterfield Transport Ltd as shown. **(5 marks)**
    b) A bus driver employed by Chesterfield Transport Ltd is having to work a high number of hours of overtime. The driver is unhappy with the situation.
       i)   Which three people could the driver approach to try and solve this problem? **(3 marks)**
       ii) Explain who might be the best person in the company to solve the driver's problem. **(6 marks)**
       iii) How might the company avoid a similar problem arising in the future? **(6 marks)**

1999

2. The Broadford Manor Hotel is a luxury hotel, with wealthy people and businesses as its main customers.
   a) What are likely to be the main aims and objectives of this hotel? **(5 marks)**
   b) Why is the hotel able to charge high prices for its accommodation? **(6 marks)**

2000

3. The 'Tesco Steering Wheel' shown is used to illustrate Tesco's objectives. The company wants each of its employees to be aware of these objectives.
   a) Suggest three suitable ways Tesco could communicate the company objectives to its employees. **(3 marks)**
   b) Select one method of communication. Briefly justify why you think it would be a good way of communicating the objectives. **(3 marks)**

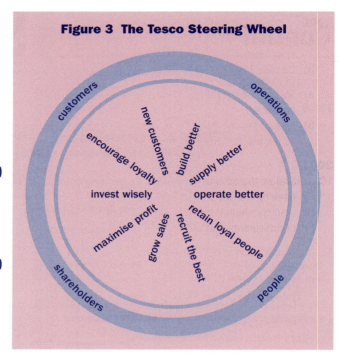

Figure 3 The Tesco Steering Wheel

4. Supermarket chains, such as Tesco, now sell services and non-food products, including bank accounts and petrol.
   a) Explain two reasons why companies move into new lines of business. **(4 marks)**
   b) State two problems selling a new product or service might create for a business. **(2 marks)**

2001

5. a) Many of McDonald's restaurants are franchised. Briefly state what is meant by a franchise.
   (2 marks)
   b) Describe two ways in which McDonald's could help franchise-owners to run their restaurants.
   (4 marks)

Higher

1998

6. a) Explain the roles and responsibilities of both directors and managers within the structure shown in Figure 2. **(8 marks)**
   b) How might trade union officials, middle managers and other employees of the company view the role of the Employee Director? **(12 marks)**

1999

7. A luxury hotel is considering two possible options for long-term expansion.
    - Building additional leisure facilities
    - Buying and renovating a row of five cottages close to the hotel.

    Discuss the likely impact of these options for expansion on the business. Giving your reasons, suggest which option the hotel management should choose. **(12 marks)**

2000

8. a) Suggest three suitable ways Tesco could communicate the company objectives to its employees.
    b) Discuss why good communications are important for the success of a company. **(6 marks)**

9. a) State two reasons why businesses might wish to expand by taking over firms producing similar products. **(2 marks)**
    b) Explain two reasons why a company like Tesco may diversify into new areas of business, such as financial services or petrol retailing. **(4 marks)**

2001

10. a) Explain the advantages to an entrepreneur of buying a McDonald's franchise, rather than opening his/her own restaurant. **(6 marks)**
    b) Discuss whether you believe McDonald's should continue to expand by increasing the number of restaurants that are franchise-owned. **(8 marks)**

11. a) Give two forms of ICT that McDonald's Head Office can use to communicate with its restaurants. **(2 marks)**
    b) Explain two reasons why it is important for McDonald's to have good communications between Head Office and its restaurants. **(4 marks)**

12. Figure 4 shows a typical organisational structure for a McDonald's restaurant. It can be seen that there are four levels in the hierarchy.
    a) Discuss whether it would be worthwhile for McDonald's to have an organisational structure on display in each of its restaurants. **(6 marks)**
    b) Consider whether McDonald's would benefit from removing one level of the hierarchy and having no assistant managers. **(8 marks)**

Figure 4 Organisation Structure of a Typical McDonald's Restaurant

Restaurant Manager

1st Assistant Manager   2nd Assistant Manager

5 Floor Managers

35 Crew Members (mainly part-time)

Business Behaviour – Marketing

SECTION 3

Foundation

1999

1. The management of a luxury hotel would like to increase the occupancy rate of the rooms (the number of rooms booked per time period). Two options are currently being considered to encourage more people to stay at the hotel.
    *   Reduce the price of rooms to compete with more cheaply priced tourist hotels in nearby towns.
    *   Increase the amount of advertising and the number of promotions.
        a) For each option, explain the possible effects on the business.   **(6 marks)**
        b) Which option might be more successful in encouraging people to stay at the hotel? Your answer should give reasons why you have chosen this option and why you have not chosen the other.   **(8 marks)**

2001

2. McDonald's is planning to open a new restaurant in a small town called Benson.
    a) Consider the reasons why McDonald's conducts market research before it decides whether to open a new restaurant.   **(6 marks)**

3. McDonald's usually spends £10,000 on promoting a new restaurant. The costs of different ways of advertising and promotion are given in the table below.

Figure 6 Possible Promotional Methods

Method	Cost
Large posters on key sites	£400 per poster per month
Local leaflet drops (flyers)	£500 per 10,000
Local newspaper advertisement	£500 per advert
Competition in local schools	£200 for prizes
Regional television	£8000 for 3 × 20-second non-peak adverts
Local radio	£1000 for 12 × 20-second adverts
Meal discount offers	£2 per meal

a) Explain why McDonald's needs to promote a new restaurant.   **(4 marks)**
b) Discuss the best ways to promote a new McDonald's using the £10,000 budget. Show exactly how you would spend this money, giving reasons for your choices.   **(8 marks)**

2002

4. Ford uses the marketing mix to persuade consumers to buy its cars.

Figure 7

Price: Ford prices cars carefully to suit a range of budgets. It recently lowered prices because it was criticised for charging more for cars in the UK than it did in Europe.

Product: Ford offers a wide range of different vehicles to suit all market segments.

Place: Most new cars are bought through showrooms. Dealerships are awarded franchises by Ford. Dealers provide other services such as repairs and servicing.

Promotion: Ford uses advertising media such as newspapers and peak time television, sponsorship, and promotions targeted at particular market segments.

a) Describe two ways in which Ford could encourage consumers to buy its cars rather than those of its competitors. **(4 marks)**

b) Briefly explain two ways in which Ford might promote a small car, such as the Ford Ka. **(4 marks)**

c) Discuss whether you believe Ford should try to sell more cars directly through the internet. **(6 marks)**

Higher

1999

5. The management of a luxury hotel is considering how best to market the hotel and its facilities to potential customers. It also wishes to increase the hotel's occupancy rate.

Suggest an appropriate marketing mix for the hotel. **(7 marks)**

6. a) Many businesses now use the internet to sell their products. State three difficulties that might be experienced with this method of selling. **(3 marks)**

b) Outline three suitable pricing strategies Tesco could use when setting its petrol prices. **(3 marks)**

2002

7. Ford operates in a competitive market. To sell its vehicles it needs to ensure that they are marketed effectively. Look at Figure 7 (boxed information).

a) Describe two reasons why market research is important to Ford.

b) Discuss how Ford might attempt to increase its share of the UK car market. **(8 marks)**

Business Behaviour – Production

SECTION 4

Foundation

2002

1. a) What is meant by 'quality control'?   **(2 marks)**
    b) Briefly describe two reasons why quality control is important to a business such as Ford.
                                                                                 (4 marks)

2. Ford has to decide just where and how its vehicles are made.

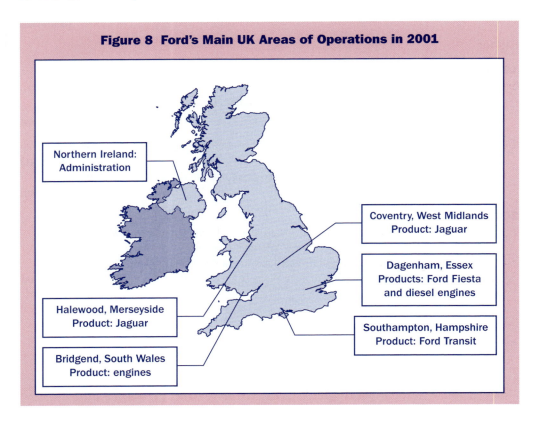

Figure 8 Ford's Main UK Areas of Operations in 2001

Northern Ireland:
Administration

Coventry, West Midlands
Product: Jaguar

Dagenham, Essex
Products: Ford Fiesta
and diesel engines

Halewood, Merseyside
Product: Jaguar

Southampton, Hampshire
Product: Ford Transit

Bridgend, South Wales
Product: engines

a) Outline two reasons why it is important that Ford spends money on research and
    development.

b) Briefly explain two reasons why most cars today are made using flow production methods.

(4 marks)

c) Discuss whether it would be better for Ford to have a single factory in the UK rather than having several throughout the country.

(6 marks)

Higher

2002

3. a) What is meant by the term 'opportunity cost'? **(2 marks)**

   b) Outline two opportunity costs faced by Ford when it develops a new model of car. **(4 marks)**

4. Ford has used flow production techniques for many years.

Describe the benefits that can be gained by Ford manufacturing cars using flow rather than batch production methods.

(6 marks)

Foundation

1999   **Figure 9**

Position	Normal Working Week	Rates/Per Hour	Overtime Rates/ Per Hour
Garage Staff	38 hours (Monday–Friday)	£5.25	Mon–Fri – £6.25 Sat – £7.20 Sun – £6.22
Bus Driver	48 hours (Monday–Saturday)	£4.98	Sun – £6.22

5. a) A mechanic has been offered 10 hours of overtime from Monday to Friday. Alternatively, the mechanic could work 7 hours on Sunday, earning an extra £63.
   i) How much would the mechanic earn from the overtime worked on Monday to Friday? You must show all your working.
   ii) Which offer of overtime might the mechanic accept? Give one reason for your answer.

   b) The Director of Finance and Administration has suggested that the company should cut back on its training to save costs. Explain why the Personnel Manager might oppose this view.

   (6 marks)

   c) What are the potential benefits to the company's employees of a nationally recognised system of qualifications?
   (5 marks)

Figure 10 Chesterfield Transport (1989) Ltd's Financial Performance 1991 to 1995

All amounts in £000s

	Year				
	1991	1992	1993	1994*	1995
Revenue	7 226	7 308	6 930	7 484	7 644
Operating Profit	380	479	241	461	277
Interest Payments	320	276	215	164	183
Net Profit	64	231	44	307	111
Current Assets	999	729	965	1 473	970
Current Liabilities	1 132	1 204	1 258	1 881	2 583

*These figures include the revenue from White's World Travel, taken over in 1994

6. By 1995, Chesterfield Transport was facing increasing competition from other local bus companies and had a number of other major problems.
    a) Comment on the company's financial performance from 1991 to 1995. Credit will be given for using calculations in your answer. **(8 marks)**
    b) As a member of the Finance Department write a report for the Board of Directors suggesting ways in which the company could improve its financial position. **(12 marks)**

7. The management of a luxury hotel is considering two possible options for long-term expansion.
    - Building additional facilities
    - The purchase and renovation of five cottages close to the hotel.
    a) Describe three sources of finance which the business might use to pay for long-term expansion. **(6 marks)**
    b) You are a business consultant. Write a report for the hotel's management explaining which of the two options for expansion you would recommend. In your report you should:
        - outline the benefits and drawbacks of each option
        - consider the effects on the hotel's costs and revenues
        - select the better option in your view, giving reasons for your choice. **(17 marks)**

8. Explain why a business, such as a hotel, might prefer to use profit to finance expansion. Use examples to illustrate your answer. **(6 marks)**

2000
9. Look at the financial information on Tesco.

Figure 11 Selected financial data from Tesco's Profit & Loss Account

	1997/8 £m	1996/7 £m
Sales (less value added tax)	16,450	13,900
Operating expenses (including profit-sharing)	15,550	13,100
Operating profit	900	800
Profit (after tax and interest payments)	505	520
Retained profit	250	295

(The figures have been rounded up/down)

    a) i) Briefly describe what happened to the amount of operating profit Tesco made between 1996/7 and 1997/8.
       ii) Explain how opening more stores for 24 hours a day could change the company's costs and revenue. **(6 marks)**

    b) Describe two factors that may be taken into account when deciding where to build a new Tesco Extra store. **(4 marks)**

2001
10. It has been suggested that Tesco should stop giving vouchers to its customers and lower its prices instead. You have been asked by Tesco's Board of Directors to investigate the possible effects of this suggestion on the business.

Write your report to the Board of Directors. In your report you should:
- consider the benefits and drawbacks of both vouchers and lower prices to Tesco
- make a recommendation on what the company should do, clearly giving your reasons.

(12 marks)

2001

11. The table below shows how much profit a typical restaurant makes in January compared with the target it was set. It can be seen that the restaurant gained more sales than its target. However, the restaurant failed to reach its net profit target for the month.
    a) Briefly state why McDonald's sets each of its restaurants a target budget. **(2 marks)**
    b) Comment on why the restaurant's revenue from food sales might have been higher than expected. **(6 marks)**
    c) If a restaurant is to make a profit it will need either to:
       - sell more food to customers, or
       - reduce the amount of money it spends to run the business.

One restaurant manager decides to save money by cutting back on the amount she spends on advertising and crew members' wages. The restaurant manager asks you to comment on her plan.

Give the restaurant manager advice on whether her plan is a good idea. **(6 marks)**

2002

Figure 12

Ford's Turnover by Area*

Turnover by area	1999 £ millions	1998 £ millions	1997 £ millions
UK	4033	4334	4369
EU Countries	1973	1931	1935
Non-EU Countries	286	443	572
Total Turnover	**6292**	**6708**	**6876**

Increased worldwide competition has caused Ford's profits to decline. The company has tried to increase the efficiency of its car production in order to reduce costs and stop the fall in its profits.

Ford's Profit and Loss Accounts*

	1999 £ millions	1998 £ millions	1997 £ millions
Turnover	6292	6708	6876
Cost of Sales	5716	5928	6167
Gross Profit	576	780	709
Expenses	544	559	529
Operating Profit	**32**	**221**	**180**

*Extracts from Ford Motor Company Ltd's accounts

12. Look at the financial figures for Ford.
    a) Describe two possible reasons for the change in sales turnover shown. **(4 marks)**
    b) Briefly explain two problems Ford could experience if its profits were to continue to fall.
       (4 marks)
    c) Discuss two possible consequences if Ford closed down its main plant at Dagenham.
       (6 marks)

Higher

1998

13. Chesterfield Transport was set up as an employee owned company in 1989. The finance to start up and purchase the company from the council was obtained through a bank loan and from selling shares to employees.

    a) What other possible sources of finance might have been used to raise the capital needed?
       (4 marks)

    b) Why might other sources of finance have been rejected in favour of a bank loan and selling shares to employees? **(6 marks)**

    c) The employees paid the council £2,450,000 for the shares. A bank loan was used to buy 85% of the shares by the holding company. The employees bought the other 15%. All 350 employees owned an equal number of shares. How much would each individual have had to contribute to the purchase of shares? You must show your working. **(3 marks)**

    d) No dividends were paid to shareholders between 1989 and 1995. Explain the possible reasons for this decision. **(5 marks)**

14. Look at the table opposite. It contains figures from the balance sheet and profit and loss account of a food supplier to the Broadford Hotel for the financial years 1998 and 1999.

    Figure 13 Table showing Profit and Loss Account of a food supplier to the Bradford Hotel

	31.5.1998 (£)	31.5.1999 (£)
Net profit	2,540,000	2,937,000
Stock	800,000	900,000
Current assets	1,100,000	1,300,000
Current liabilities	700,000	600,000
Capital employed	25,400,000	26,700,000

    a) Calculate the following ratios for each year. You must show all your working.
       i)   The return on capital employed (ROCE)
       ii) The current ratio
       iii) The acid test ratio **(6 marks)**
    b) Compare the ratios and explain whether this business has improved its performance on profitability and liquidity. **(6 marks)**

2000

15. Tesco is considering increasing the number of its superstores which remain open for 24 hours a day.

    As a management consultant, write a report to Tesco's board of Directors explaining the arguments both for and against such a move. Your report should contain a recommendation on whether the company should continue to extend opening hours. **(18 marks)**

16. Look at the tables in Figure 12.
    a) Explain the problems Ford might experience if its profits continue to fall. **(6 marks)**
    b) In October 2000, Ford announced major price cuts. Discuss how this might have affected Ford's profits. **(8 marks)**

People and Organisations

SECTION 6

Foundation

1998

1. Companies often provide training opportunities for their employees. What are the benefits to a company of providing training? **(6 marks)**

1999

2. Most of the employees of Chesterfield Transport Ltd belong to a trade union.
   a) What is meant by a trade union? **(2 marks)**
   b) Why might employees wish to belong to a trade union? **(4 marks)**

2000

3. Tesco recruits most of its employees through job centres.
   a) i) Give two reasons why Tesco chooses to use Job Centres to recruit new staff. **(2 marks)**
      ii) Describe how Tesco might select suitable new employees from those who apply for jobs. **(4 marks)**
      iii) Describe the training Tesco might provide for a new employee joining the company. Briefly explain why the training is needed. **(6 marks)**
   b) As well as paying wages to its employees, Tesco also offers them benefits such as staff discounts and profit sharing.

   Briefly discuss why Tesco gives each of these two benefits to its employees. **(6 marks)**

2001

4. McDonald's is planning to open a new restaurant in a small town called Benson. It will need to recruit new crew members for this restaurant.
   a) Explain two reasons why McDonald's might want to employ young people to work in the restaurant.
   (4 marks)
   b) Explain two methods McDonald's uses to motivate its crew members
   c) Discuss what training would be needed by crew members when they first start to work at a restaurant.

Foundation & Higher

1999

5. Running a luxury hotel is very labour intensive. The hotel management has found recruiting and retaining staff a major problem.

   a) What is meant by the term 'labour intensive'? **(2 marks)**

   b) Suggest how the management of a luxury hotel could overcome recruitment and staffing problems.
   (6 marks)

   c) Discuss how each of your suggestions might affect the profitability of the hotel. **(8 marks)**

2002

6. a) What is meant by the term 'redundancy'? **(2 marks)**

   b) Briefly explain two reasons why a firm might need to make workers redundant. **(4 marks)**

7. Ford has had problems with the number of days employees missed from work. Ford has tried to reduce the rate of absenteeism by giving workers a bonus if attendance improves.

Imagine that you are an employment consultant and you have been asked by Ford to consider other ways of reducing the number of days employees are absent from work.

You need to write a report to the Human Resources Manager at Ford that:
- Outlines two or three possible ways of reducing the number of days employees take off work. You should show clearly how each suggestion would work.
- Discusses the problems Ford might have in carrying out these suggestions.
- Gives a clear recommendation on which action you think would have the best chance of success in reducing absenteeism. Your recommendation should be based on the points made in your discussion.

(17 marks)

Higher

2000

8. High labour turnover is a problem in the retailing industry.
   a) Explain two reasons why a high rate of labour turnover can cause difficulties for retailers such as Tesco.

   (4 marks)

   b) Briefly discuss two methods Tesco might use to help reduce its rate of labour turnover. **(6 marks)**

9. Tesco has expanded both at home and overseas.

Figure 14 Tesco's Stores, 1998

	Number of Stores	Sales (£m)
Ireland*	109	1 028
France	103	644
Hungary	43	57
Poland	31	22
Czech Republic	6	84
Slovakia	7	61
United Kingdom	534	14,640
Total	**833**	**16,536**

* Northern Ireland and the Republic of Ireland

a) Look at the table shown and calculate the average sales per store in both Poland and France.

(4 marks)

b) Comment on the possible reasons for the difference between the two values that you have calculated.

(6 marks)

c) Retailers such as Tesco experience problems running stores in the UK. Discuss three additional problems that might arise from operating stores overseas. **(9 marks)**

10. Like any successful business, McDonald's needs to have a well-motivated work force.
    a) Explain two methods McDonald's can use to motivate their staff. **(4 marks)**
    b) Comment on the suitability of your suggestions by referring to the work of one of the following theorists:
       - Maslow
       - Mayo
       - McGregor. **(8 marks)**

Aiding and Controlling Business Activity

SECTION 7

Foundation

1999

1. How might a luxury hotel business be affected if standards of living in the UK are increasing?   **(6 marks)**

2002

2. Both the government and the economy can influence the success of a business like Ford.
    a) Explain two ways in which high interest rates might affect the demand for Ford's vehicles.   **(4 marks)**
    b) Explain two ways in which Ford might be affected if the government were to pass stricter laws on how much pollution vehicles were allowed to create.   **(4 marks)**
    c) Discuss how the UK's membership of the European Union affects Ford.   **(6 marks)**

Foundation & Higher

1998

3. In 1985 the Government made local councils change the way they ran their bus operations.
    a) What was the main reason for this change?   **(2 marks)**
    b) Chesterfield Council set up its own bus company which moved into profit after one year. Suggest how this might have been achieved.   **(6 marks)**
    c) Explain the advantages to the local council of selling its bus company to a management buy-out in 1989.   **(6 marks)**

Higher

1999

4. The Broadford Manor Hotel is a luxury hotel.
    a) What are the main aims and objectives of this business likely to be?   **(5 marks)**
    b) The Broadford Manor Hotel wants to take over the Broadford Golf Club. Discuss the benefits and problems that such a takeover might bring.   **(8 marks)**
    c) How might a recession in the United Kingdom economy affect the business?   **(6 marks)**

2002

5. Both the government and the economy can influence the success of a business like Ford.
    a) Explain how a strong pound could have led Ford to stop production at Dagenham for a period of three weeks in 1999.   **(6 marks)**
    b) Discuss whether Ford benefits from the UK being a member of the European Union.   **(8 marks)**

PART FIVE

SAMPLE QUESTIONS FOR AQA 'B'

Specification B

SECTION 1

For Specification B, there are a number of possible examination routes. These are:

Full course: Paper 1, Coursework, Paper 3

Full course: Paper 1, Paper 2, Paper 3

Short course: Paper 1, Coursework

Short course: Paper 1, Paper 2.

Paper 1

A Case Study is issued with Paper 1. It contains enough information to allow you to answer the questions. Again it is told as a 'story'. It is given to you as an insert so that you can easily read it through before looking at the questions. To help you, the information is usually numbered or lettered so that you know which pieces to refer to for each question.

Paper 2

This is the examination alternative to coursework. It therefore does not test 'knowledge', but rather, the skills of analysis, application and evaluation that would be tested by coursework. There is a Case Study issued with the examination; this consists of a single question (often broken down into parts), an example of which is given on page 161.

Paper 3

This does not have a Case Study approach. Small items of stimulus information are used on which to base the questions. Examples of questions are given on page 169.

Data A

Josie Wales has worked in the Red Lion public house as catering manager for three years. She has built up the catering side of the business by concentrating on events catering, for example, weddings and funerals. The Red Lion has recently been taken over and no longer wants to sell food so Josie has been made redundant. She has decided that she would like to start her own catering business.

1. Why might Josie have decided she wants to set up her own business? **(12 marks)**

Data B

Josie decided that she would become an outside caterer. What this means is that she would provide the catering for events such as weddings and parties. She realised that she would need premises on which to do the preparation and cooking, equipment, a van to transport the food, and crockery and cutlery for serving it.

Josie decided that she would need to find out about the market for her service and so produced a questionnaire. She asked the questions of 50 people in her home village.

2. Josie decided that she had some start-up costs and some running costs and tried to list them. Explain why it would be difficult for Josie to divide costs in this way and give examples to support your answer. **(6 marks)**

3. Explain why the results of Josie's market research may be unreliable. **(4 marks)**

4. Suggest other forms of market research that Josie could have undertaken. Explain which would be more effective, and why. **(6 marks)**

Data C

Josie looked at the findings of her market research and thought that a market for her service **did** exist. She calculated the various costs and decided that she would need more money than she herself had. A friend advised her to prepare a business plan.

5. Explain why Josie would need to prepare a business plan. **(4 marks)**

6. Suggest the main contents that would have to go in the business plan. **(8 marks)**

Data D

Josie needed to invest £20,000 to start the business. She calculated that she would need an overdraft facility at her bank. She thought this would be in the region of £3,000. Josie had £12,000 of her own money and would need a medium term bank loan for the remainder.

Josie looked forward to being her own boss and decided to set up the business as a sole trader. She was aware of the risks of this but also thought that it had many advantages.

Josie had fairly modest aims for the business. She hoped to at least breakeven, and maybe make a small profit, by the end of Year 1.

7. Explain how Josie's objectives might alter in the future. **(8 marks)**

8. Explain why Josie might need an overdraft facility. **(5 marks)**

9. Josie asked for a medium term loan. Explain what this means and how it is different to short and long term loans. **(6 marks)**

10. Josie was looking forward to being her own boss. This is just one benefit of being a sole trader. Explain the other benefits and the drawbacks of operating as a sole trader. **(12 marks)**

Data E

Profit and Loss Account

	31/3/2002	31/3/2003
Sales revenue	£40,000	£48,000
Cost of sales	£16,000	£19,200
Expenses	£20,000	£21,000

11. Look at the profit and loss account and calculate:
    - Gross profit to sales revenue for 2003
    - Net profit to sales revenue for 2003.

    Show your working. **(10 marks)**

12. Do you think that Josie's business has improved over the two years? Give reasons for your answer. **(10 marks)**

Data F

Food scare!

The local hospital has reported several cases of food poisoning and is trying to find out its source. Although there are now 14 cases, it is not clear that they have all eaten the same thing, so investigations are ongoing. A hospital spokesman said 'Although we do not yet have any evidence, I feel that this could be due to outside catering. The last time we had an outbreak of this size, all the victims had been to a wedding and had eaten fish that had not been stored at the correct temperature'

13. How might Josie's business be affected by the report in the local paper? **(5 marks)**

Data G

Josie's business has a good reputation and picks up a lot of business from recommendations. She has particularly targeted smaller events that take place in homes, rather than large weddings etc. The small events include birthday parties, dinner parties, garden parties and barbecues. She now feels that she needs to market her services more widely, so she has employed a marketing consultant to help her.

14. You are acting as the marketing consultant and need to advise Josie of the best marketing mix for her business. You should advise Josie on all aspects of the marketing mix. **(15 marks)**

Specification B Case Study Examples for Paper 2

SECTION 3

BURNSIDE BOARDING KENNELS

Instructions to candidates

- Time allowed: 1 hour.
- You are advised to spend 15 minutes in
  - reading the task
  - reading through all the data in the case study
  - identifying parts of the data that you might use in your written report.
- Writing up your report should take up to 45 minutes.

Task

Read through all of the data. Using your knowledge and understanding of business, write a report covering the following:

Burnside Boarding Kennels has suffered falling profits over the last three years. Morag Argyll, who runs the kennels, has asked you to write a report advising her on the nature of the problem and the best action to solve it.

- Explain the possible reasons for the fall in profits suffered by Burnside Kennels.
- Suggest ways in which the business could increase its profits. Explain why each way might be successful.
- Advise Morag Argyll on the best action to improve the profits from the kennels. Give **detailed** reasons for your selection.
- Explain what further information you would want to receive to help improve your advice on the best action.

Your report will be assessed on your ability to:

	Marks
select and use data	24
interpret the data and apply your business studies understanding	16
evaluate evidence, make reasoned judgements and present accurate and appropriate conclusions	16
spell, punctuate and use the rules of grammar accurately.	3
Total	59

Background

Burnside Boarding Kennels has been in the business of looking after people's dogs for over 20 years. The kennels are situated on the outskirts of Linchester, which is a popular tourist resort.

The business is owned by Morag Argyll, who runs the kennels with a qualified part-time helper.

Burnside was at one time a farm, but the fields are now rented out, except for an area growing Christmas trees. The kennels occupy the old farm buildings which have been suitably converted. (See map.)

Profits from the business have decreased in the past three years, mainly because of falling revenue from the kennels.

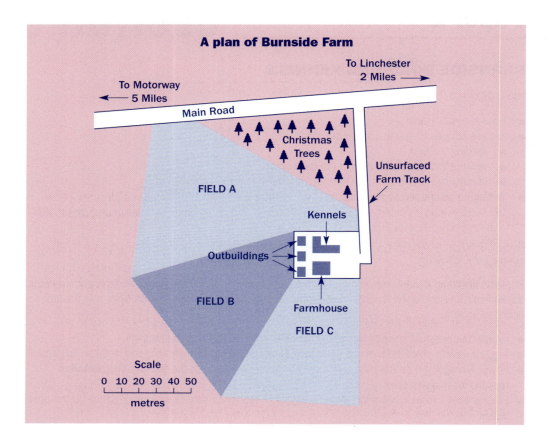

A plan of Burnside Farm

To Linchester
2 Miles →

To Motorway
← 5 Miles

Main Road

Christmas Trees

FIELD A

Unsurfaced Farm Track

Kennels

Outbuildings

FIELD B

Farmhouse

FIELD C

Scale

0 10 20 30 40 50

metres

BURNSIDE BOARDING KENNELS

Profit and Loss Account for 1997

EXPENDITURE	£	INCOME	£
Dog food	4 000	Kennel fees	27 000
Wages of part-time worker	5 000	Rent from fields	6 000
Morag Argyll's wages	12 000	Sales of Christmas trees	3 000
Overheads	9 000		
Profit	6 000		
	36 000		36 000

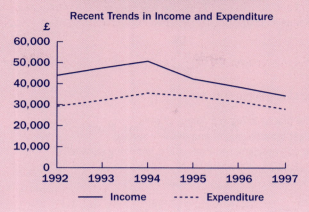

BURNSIDE BOARDING KENNEL

Recent Trends in Income and Expenditure

—— Income   ----- Expenditure

Market potential and market share

In Linchester and the surrounding countryside there are about 10,000 houses. Linchester is in the middle of an attractive rural area. An increasing number of tourists are being attracted to the area, exploring the countryside and various historical sites.

A magazine for dog owners recently published the results of a national survey which showed that 25% of households owned a dog and that, of the dog-owning households, about 40% put their dogs in kennels for an average of one week a year. Almost 10% of dog owners also owned a cat, while 20% owned small pets such as rabbits, hamsters and goldfish.

At Burnside each dog is kept in a 'cell'. There are 20 cells available for 50 weeks of the year. Burnside charge £6 per dog per day. An analysis of past bookings shows that:

75% of Burnside's business is during the summer months.

60% of Burnside's customers have used the kennels more than three times over the last four years.

10% of Burnside's customers use the kennels more than twice a year.

Burnside's marketing

To advertise Burnside, Morag has a signpost facing the main road at the end of the farm track. She also has the kennels listed in Yellow Pages. Finally, as she says, 'I have a lot of repeat business and therefore rely on word of mouth to promote my business'.

Market research

Morag carried out a local telephone survey to find out what the most important factors were when people were deciding which kennels to choose. She asked people to rank the following factors in order of importance: price, convenient location, good facilities, well-qualified staff. The results of the survey are set out overleaf.

Factor	Percentage of people putting this as first choice
Price	20%
Convenient location	10%
Good facilities	40%
Qualified staff	30%

Other comments that Morag noted included:

- the need for places to leave a variety of pets
- some interest for a collection and delivery service
- interest for dog obedience classes and a grooming service.

Competition

Three years ago another kennels, called Petslodge, opened nearer the centre of Linchester. They are about the same size as Burnside. Recently Petslodge has been running an advertising campaign. The following advertisement has been used as part of its publicity.

Tender loving care for your best friend provided by

PETSLODGE

KENNELS & CATTERY

Boarding available all year round for your cat or dog

Heated Kennels
Individual covered runs
Dogs walked daily

10424 610379

Dolwelly Road, Linchester

NEWMAN CAFÉS LTD

Ray and Pat Newman have owned and run Newman Cafés Ltd for over 10 years. The company operates a small chain of five cafés located in five towns, all within 30 miles of each other (see Data 4). Each café offers the same basic menu of a range of snacks together with hot and cold drinks. Although the company continues to make a reasonable profit from the cafés, Ray and Pat are keen both to expand and to increase profit. They do not want to go into the fast-food market of burger and pizza bars. Instead, having noticed the success of some of the leading coffee chains in London, they are considering changing their cafés into a more upmarket coffee chain. Ray and Pat intend to establish a name and reputation in their area long before the major companies expand into the region.

Your task

If Ray and Pat are to change the business from cafés to a coffee chain, they will need to consider how to finance the development and how to make their chain competitive. Ray and Pat need to write a report to present to their business adviser before continuing with their plans. Use the data and your knowledge and understanding of business to write a report that Ray and Pat could use. Your report should include:

- the possible reasons for developing the coffee chain
- how this development might be financed
- what additional information Ray and Pat will need to collect about their possible competitors
- given the likely future arrival of leading coffee chains to the region, explain how Ray and Pat could compete with these larger businesses.

Your report will be assessed on your ability to:

	Marks
select and use data	24
interpret the data and apply your business studies understanding	16
evaluate evidence, make reasoned judgements and present accurate and appropriate conclusions	16
spell, punctuate and use the rules of grammar accurately.	3
Total	59

Study all the information before you begin your task.

Data 1 Extract from a newspaper report on the expansion plans of leading coffee chains

It's a Coffee War!

Upmarket coffee chains are battling to capture a market currently worth over £500 million a year. This is set to triple in the next five years. There are already well over 700 coffee shops across the country, although London has the greatest concentration – at the moment. Firms make around 25p profit from an average price of £1.50 a cup. Competition between the firms is rarely linked to price: quality snacks, image and atmosphere are significant marketing factors that build on the core product – **coffee!**

You can choose from:

Americano:	an expresso with steamed water
Con panna:	an expresso with whipped cream
Dry:	with extra foam
Harmless:	skimmed milk
Macchiato:	an expresso with foamed milk
Latte:	expresso with steamed or foamed milk
Moccha:	expresso, chocolate syrup, steamed milk and whipped cream

Market analysts report that 1999 saw coffee replacing tea as Britain's favourite away-from-home drink. The craze for different coffee drinks is set to be one of the biggest retail success stories of the millennium.

Data 2 Who are the major coffee chains?

Coffee Chain	Existing coffee shops	Expansion plans
Starbucks	136 outlets in the UK, 77 of them in London	It aims to double outlets by 2003.
Pret a Manger	100 sandwich shops in the UK, 75 of which are in London.	Opening 50 shops over the next two years and a doubling in size by 2005.
Costa	200 shops, 100 of which are in London	It plans to diversify with sandwiches and coffee shops in other retail outlets.
Coffee Republic	65 shops, 40 of which are in London.	It has started a revamp of its stores and is giving its image a national facelift.
Aroma	37 shops, 28 located in London.	It has plans to increase shops to 50 by the end of 2000 with many more shops to be opened outside London in 2001.

Chart showing estimated market share in August 2000

Pret a Manger 12%
Costa 20%
Coffee Republic 10%
Aroma 7%
Other outlets 31%
Starbucks 20%

Data 3 Newman's typical menu for its existing cafés

Menu

Tea £0.90

Coffee £1.10

Soft drinks *from* £1.00 *per glass*

Sandwiches *from* £1.50

Cakes *from* £1.20 *for scone & butter*

Pastries *from* £0.80 *for a sausage roll*

Opening hours 09.30 to 17.00

Data 4 Map showing the location of Newman's cafés

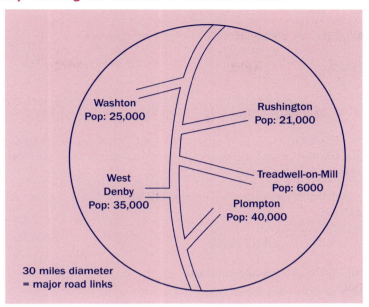

Washton
Pop: 25,000

Rushington
Pop: 21,000

West
Denby
Pop: 35,000

Treadwell-on-Mill
Pop: 6000

Plompton
Pop: 40,000

30 miles diameter
= major road links

Data 5 Key economic and social figures for the area in which Newman Cafés Ltd operated in 2000

Unemployment rate for the area averaged 3.1 %

Unemployment rate for the UK averaged 3.7%

Average gross weekly earnings for the area = £445

Average gross weekly earnings for the UK = £389

Average expenditure on food and drink eaten outside the home (excluding alcohol) in £s per person per week in the area = £6.50

Average expenditure on food and drink eaten outside the home (excluding alcohol) in £s per person per week in the UK = £5.20

Data 6 Key financial figures for Newman Cafés Ltd over the last three years

(for the financial year ended)

	04/2001	04/2000	04/1999
Sales Revenue	£900,000	£896,900	£890,590
Gross Profit	£540,000	£547,100	£552,160
Net Profit	£90,000	£98,659	£106,870

Retained profit available for Newman Cafés Ltd in April 2001 is £60,000

Data 7 Sources of finance used for the existing five cafés

Shareholders' Capital:	£200,000
Past Profit:	£150,000
Medium-term bank loan:	£100,000

Data 8 Estimated costs and timescale for re-development of Newman's five cafés

*Total Costs for re-developing **each** café*

Interior changes including decoration and equipment: £25,000
New furniture: £15,000
Exterior changes to cafés: £10,000
Uniforms, menus and other sundries: £4000

Timescale

Each café would be closed in turn for two weeks, so that all work would be completed within ten weeks

Data 9 Typical advertising costs for the area in which Newman Cafés Ltd. operates

Local Free Newspaper: Half-page advert £100

Regional Evening Newspaper: Half-page advert £2100

Regional Daily Newspaper: Half-page advert £1400

Local Commercial Radio: broadcasting a 30-second advertisement £300

Regional ITV broadcasting: a 30-second advertisement £10,000 before 1800 hours, £15,000 to £30,000 after 1800

Specification B
Sample Questions for
Paper 3

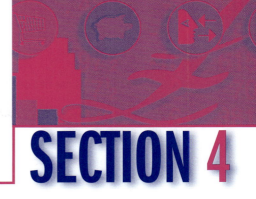

SECTION 4

This is a selection of typical data and typical questions. The 2001 material is taken from the Specimen paper produced by the examination board.

THE EXTERNAL ENVIRONMENT OF BUSINESS

Figure 15 Fleetmore journal

'TOWN ATTRACTS £4 MILLION INVESTMENT'

A Canadian company which produces parts for cars, announced last week that is is setting up a new factory in Fleetmoor. Carcomps will be making driver air bags for leading European car companies. The company is taking over a large industrial unit on Fleetmoor's Business Park.

Mr Hill, Managing Director of Carcomps said, 'The company has spent a great deal of time and effort searching for the right location. In the end, we were impressed by the quality of Fleetmoor's Business Park, its buildings and the ease of access to European markets. There is a good workforce in the Fleetmoor area and an established car industry. Finally, we were impressed by the team-work of the local councils and agencies negotiating with us'.

---

200 NEW JOBS

Councillor Rowland, who chairs Fleetmoor's Economic Development Committee, commented, 'These 200 jobs give us the start we need to reach our target of 2500 new jobs by the Year 2000. With unemployment in Fleetmoor running at 12%, due to the decline of the local mining and engineering industries, the arrival of Carcomps is just the boost we need. The Council has been working hard to improve the road network and to provide financial help for new firms. Our worldwide telecommunication links are second to none in the region'.

A Government minister stated, 'This is an important development for the northern region and for the UK as a whole. Greater investment will help create jobs and trade, and will give people confidence for the future.'

Foundation

1997

1. a) Explain why Carcomps has decided that Fleetmoor is a suitable location for its new factory.
   (10 marks)
   b) The Fleetmoor Business park is an Enterprise Zone. What is an Enterprise Zone?   **(5 marks)**
   c) Describe the possible social benefits and the possible social costs to Fleetmoor from this development.   **(10 marks)**
   d) Explain why this is an important development for the Northern region.   **(8 marks)**

1997

2. a) Explain why Carcomps has decided that Fleetmoor is a suitable location for its new factory.

    (10 marks)

    b) The Fleetmoor Business park is an Enterprise Zone. Why are Enterprise Zones created by the government? **(5 marks)**
    c) Explain the possible social costs to Fleetmoor of Carcomps new factory. **(9 marks)**
    d) Explain why the arrival of Carcomps is likely to be an important development for the Northern region and for the UK. **(8 marks)**

Figure 16 OLD FASHIONED BATHS
AT OLD FASHIONED PRICES!

Our independent status and huge buying capacity enable us to pass tremendous savings on to you, our customer. Call in today at our massive out-of-town showroom and warehouse and see our tremendous range of Victorian-style bathrooms.

THE OLD BATH TUB COMPANY

Alde Mill
Nr Welford   Tel: 0001222 22211 for a brochure

View our wide range of products at our web site www.btub.co.uk

---

Foundation

2002

3. a) Explain how bulk buying enables the Old Bath Tub Company to reduce its costs. **(4 marks)**
    b) Explain the advantages to the Old Bath Tub Company of having an out-of-town showroom and warehouse. **(8 marks)**
    c) Describe the benefits to the Old Bath Tub Company of having a website. **(12 marks)**

Higher

2002

4. a) The Old Bath Tub Company is considering replacing its out of town showroom and warehouse with a number of smaller, city centre shops. Explain the factors it would need to investigate before making this change. **(8 marks)**

BUSINESS STRUCTURE, ORGANISATION AND CONTROL

Foundation

1998

1. Figure 17 shows the organisational structure of Wansdyke, a manufacturing company.
    a) using examples from the chart, explain the following terms:
        - chain of command
        - span of control
        - delegation of decisions. **(9 marks)**

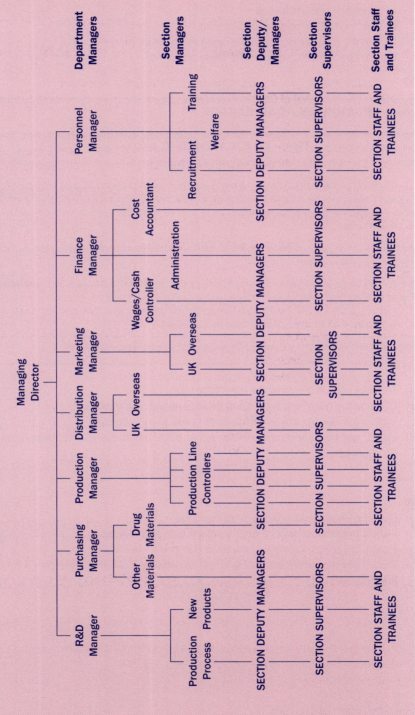

Figure 17 CHART OF WANSDYKE'S ORGANISATIONAL STRUCTURE

b) Wansdyke has identified some possible problems with its structure. These include:
- the number of managers
- roles and responsibilities
- communication and decision-making.

Explain the possible problems the company might be experiencing. **(10 marks)**

c) Explain how Wansdyke might solve these problems. **(8 marks)**

2000

Figure 18 WICKLEY ROAD GARAGE

Brian Fox is the owner of Wickley Road Garage. Wickley Road Garage opened for business in 1963 operating from a small site close to the centre of the small town of Welchurch. When the garage first opened, the main part of its business was the repair and servicing of family cars. Additional revenue came from the sale of petrol and diesel.

In 1970, building on his success in servicing cars, Brian Fox decided to expand his business by opening a franchise selling new Renault cars. Brian chose Renault as he felt that they provided successful advertising and good cars, together with advice and training for his staff. Sales of new cars from Brian's garage reached a peak in 1996, but have since declined.

In 1998 a new out-of-town Superstore opened on the outskirts of Welchurch. It also sells petrol and diesel but at a lower price than Brian's garage.

At the kiosk where customers pay for petrol and diesel, sweets, drinks and newspapers have sold well. Brian has investigated ways of increasing turnover and decided to convert part of the garage forecourt into a larger retail shop. He is proposing to sell a range of basic foods, magazines, newspapers, cards, flowers, plants, sweets and small gifts. The shop will have the same opening hours as his garage.

Brian is particularly keen to attract more customers from outside the town of Welchurch.

---

2. a) Describe what is meant by the term 'franchise'. **(4 marks)**
    b) Describe the possible advantage to Brian of operating a franchise. **(8 marks)**
    c) Explain the reasons why you think Brian is now keen to diversify. **(8 marks)**
    d) Explain why the superstore is able to sell its petrol and diesel at lower prices than Wickley Road Garage. **(6 marks)**

Higher

2000

3. a) Describe what is meant by the term 'franchise'. **(4 marks)**
    b) Explain the disadvantages that Brian might face as a franchisee. **(8 marks)**
    c) Explain the reasons why you think Brian is now keen to diversify. **(8 marks)**
    d) Explain why the superstore is able to sell its petrol and diesel at lower prices than Wickley Road Garage. **(6 marks)**

The Garage has the following opening hours:

- Monday 8 a.m. to 6 p.m.
- Saturday/Sunday 9 a.m. to 5 p.m.

Brian is concerned about the competition from the superstore and his need to increase the revenue of his business. He is re-thinking the opening hours of the shop so that it becomes more typical of a convenience store.

e) Discuss the advantages and disadvantages of having longer opening hours. **(9 marks)**

2002

Figure 19

Mildred's Ice Cream Farm is one of the best-known tourist attractions in Willshire.

Visitors are welcomed to the farm all year round. They can watch Mildred's herd of pedigree Jersey cows being milked. They can then see the milk being made into ice cream in a modern hygienic dairy.

The ice cream has a seasonal demand with peak sales between May and September. To overcome this problem, Mildred's Ice Cream Farm began producing luxury chocolates in October 2000. These chocolates are a particularly useful product as their peak sales are at Christmas and St Valentine's Day (14 February).

Mildred's Ice Cream Farm is considering other ways it could expand its business. One way it is considering is setting up a franchise operation selling ice cream through franchisees across the region.

4. a) Explain the possible reasons why Mildred's Ice Cream Farm chose to diversify from just making ice cream. **(9 marks)**
   b) Explain, using examples, the meaning of the term 'franchise'. **(6 marks)**
   c) Describe the possible advantages of being a franchisee for Mildred's Ice Cream **(6 marks)**

Higher

2002

5. a) Describe the possible advantages of being a franchisee for Mildred's Ice Cream. **(6 marks)**
   b) Discuss whether you think Mildred's Ice Cream farm should start a franchise operation. In your answer you should consider the advantages and disadvantages of franchising. **(12 marks)**

MARKETING

Foundation

1997

1. a) Sarah Clarke has been running a flower shop for just over a year. She believes that her business could be more profitable and is considering three ways to increase revenue:
   - a small advertising campaign using a leaflet drop and advertisements in a local newspaper

- a link up with local hotels to provide flowers for special occasions such as conferences and weddings
- selling additional product lines such as greetings cards, flower vases and potted plants.

Describe the advantages and disadvantages of each of these possible actions. You may also consider alternative ideas of your own. **(12 marks)**

b) Describe which action you think would be best for Sarah, giving reasons for your decision.

(3 marks)

Higher

1997

2. a) Advise Sarah on the best course of action. You may also give advice on alternative ideas of your own. **(15 marks)**

Foundation

2000

3. Look at Figure 18.
   a) Brian is keen to attract more customers from Welchurch. To promote his shop he is thinking about the following options:
      - advertising in a local newspaper
      - roadside signs advertising a range of products
      - giving 'money off' coupons, for use in the shop, to people having their car serviced.

   Consider each of the options and explain which you think would best help Brian to achieve his objective. **(15 marks)**

2000

4. Look at Figure 16.
   a) Explain why the Old Bath Tub Company might have chosen to use a persuasive rather than informative advertisement. **(10 marks)**

2001

5. Mega Music is a national chain of music stores.

Figure 20

We are opening our new Megastore in three months time. My job is to choose the most effective methods of advertising the new Megastore. I am considering:

- Direct mail
- Advertising on buses
- Local radio.

a) Consider each of these methods and advise how best to advertise the new store.

PRODUCTION

Foundation

1997

1. a) Mark clearly on the diagram where you think PCs are on the product life cycle. **(1 mark)**

   b) Explain why you have made this decision. **(4 marks)**

   c) Some PC manufacturers are cutting prices, others upgrade hardware but keep the original price. Retailers offer credit deals and free software. Advice helplines and extended guarantees are often given. Explain three ways in which businesses are trying to extend the product life cycle of PCs. **(9 marks)**

Figure 21

The market for Personal Computers (PCs) seems to have reached saturation. All manufacturers are reporting a drop in demand with no obvious sign of improvement. The major retailers are finding it increasingly difficult to sell existing stock. Competition is intense.

From a magazine article

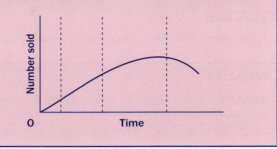

PRODUCT LIFE CYCLE FOR PERSONAL COMPUTERS

Higher

1997

2. a) Explain why businesses identify the possible product life cycle for their products. **(5 marks)**

   b) Some PC manufacturers are cutting prices, others upgrade hardware but keep the original price. Retailers offer credit deals and free software. Advice helplines and extended guarantees are often given. These offers are widely advertised.
   Advise the businesses on the possible effectiveness of these methods. **(12 marks)**

Foundation

Figure 22

Wansdyke is a pharmaceutical company producing a wide range of medicines and related products. Some of its products are manufactured using batch production methods and others using flow production methods. One major product line is an artificial sweetener, which is sold both to the food industry and direct to the public. At the moment, the artificial sweetener is produced using batch methods.

To achieve the highest quality standards, Wansdyke operates a total quality management system on all parts of the production processes.

1998

3. a) What is batch production? **(3 marks)**

   b) Why might flow production be a better system for the manufacture of artificial sweeteners? **(6 marks)**

   c) What is meant by a total quality management system? **(4 marks)**

   d) Why is it important for Wansdyke to produce high-quality products? **(8 marks)**

1998

4. a) Why might Wansdyke use both batch and flow production methods in the manufacture of its product range? **(9 marks)**
    b) Why might a total quality management system be the best way for Wansdyke to control the quality on all its production processes? **(8 marks)**

FINANCE

Foundation

> ### Figure 23
>
> Since 1991, Sarah Clarke has run a small market stall in Whitelea selling flowers to the public on Fridays and Saturdays. Her main costs are an operating licence fee paid to the local council, the hire of a van on the two days, her wages and the cost of the flowers.
>
> Sarah estimates that her fixed costs amount to £250 for the two days. On average the variable cost of each bunch of flowers is £1.35. The average price she charges for a bunch of flowers is £2.60.

1997

1. a) Using examples, explain the terms:
    - fixed costs
    - variable costs. **(6 marks)**
    b) Calculate Sarah's break-even point for the two days. Show your working. **(8 marks)**
    c) What does a break-even point show? **(2 marks)**
    d) Why is it important for Sarah to control her costs? **(4 marks)**
    e) Sarah decided to sell flowers full time through a rented shop. She prepared a business plan. Describe the main items Sarah should have in her business plan. **(10 marks)**

> ### Figure 24
>
> Sarah leased the shop and purchased a small van. Her start-up costs were as she expected, but she found that running costs were greater than estimated.
>
> Sarah opened the flower shop in time for Easter 1996.
>
> At the end of her first 12 months in the shop, Sarah reviews some of her key financial figures.
>
> | | |
> |---|---|
> | Revenue | £65,000 |
> | Cost of Sales | £35,000 |
> | Expenses – Rent | £2,400 |
> | Power | £600 |
> | Business & Water Rates | £1,200 |
> | Wages of part-time employee | £3,000 |
> | Transport | £700 |
> | Interest on loans | £900 |
> | Other | £5,200 |

f) Using examples, explain the terms:
- cost of sales
- running costs
- start-up costs. **(9 marks)**

g) Showing your workings, calculate Sarah's:
- gross profit
- net profit. **(8 marks)**

(h) How could Sarah decide how well the shop performed over the first 12 months? **(6 marks)**

Higher

1997

2. a) Calculate Sarah's break-even point for two days. Show your working. **(8 marks)**

   b) How will calculating the break-even point help Sarah to run her business? **(6 marks)**

   c) Why is it sometimes difficult to distinguish between fixed costs and variable costs? Illustrate your answer with examples. **(4 marks)**

   d) Sarah decided to sell flowers full time through a rented shop. She prepared a business plan. Explain how producing the business plan would help Sarah. **(8 marks)**

   Refer to Figure 24.

   e) Showing your workings, calculate Sarah's:
   - gross profit to sales revenue ratio
   - net profit to sales revenue ratio. **(10 marks)**

   f) How can Sarah use these ratios to assess her shop's performance over the first 12 months? **(6 marks)**

Foundation

2002

Look at Figure 19.

3. a) The following data is extracted from the accounts of Mildred's Ice Cream Farm for 2001.
   Net profit £225,000
   Sales Revenue £900,000.
   Showing your working, calculate the net profit to sales ratio for 2001. **(5 marks)**

   b) Explain what this ratio shows the owners of Mildred's Ice Cream Farm. **(4 marks)**

Higher

4. a) Study the figures from the accounts of Mildred's Ice Cream Farm.

	1999	2000	2001
Net Profit	£80,000	£144,000	£225,000
Sales Revenue	£560,000	£720,000	£900,000

Explain how the profitability of Mildred's Ice Cream Farm has changed between 1999 and 2001. Use calculations and ratios to support your answer. **(12 marks)**

Figure 25a TREMLOWS HALL

In 1996 David and Julia Watts became increasingly concerned about the cost of living in their large house. They felt that the time had come for it to 'pay its way'. David had recently retired from his job and Julia had always enjoyed preparing meals for their large family.

Now that the children had left home they had four double bedrooms that could be let as luxury bed and breakfast accommodation. They decided to call their bed and breakfast business Tremlows Hall.

They have been advised by a bank manager that in order to make a success of this business they need to produce a business plan.

EXTRACT FROM BUSINESS PLAN

TREMLOWS HALL

OWNERS	David and Julia Watts
ADDRESS	Tremlows Hall Whitfield Southshire SY13 1AL
TEL	11880 982 832
EXPERIENCE	Management experience in industry and domestic experience of looking after a large family house.
QUALIFICATIONS	Management diploma

Figure 25b

After their first summer Julia and David have not reached their break-even point. Discussing the problem they arrive at three possible solutions:

- Increase the price of each room to £55 per night.
- Target a different market and increase the price to £55 per night. Include in the package, flowers and a bottle of wine for the guests in each room (adding £5 to the variable costs per room).
- Increase the advertising from once a season to monthly, adding £1000 to the yearly fixed costs.

a) David and Julia have chosen to set up a bed and breakfast business. Explain why this particular business is suitable for them. **(12 marks)**

b) In addition to the details in the extract, describe other information the business plan should include. **(6 marks)**

c) Explain how useful a business plan will be to David and Julia. **(12 marks)**

d) Calculate how many nights the four bedrooms would need to be fully booked for the business to break even. **(10 marks)**

e) If after the first year David and Julia were not reaching their break-even point, suggest ways of improving their situation. **(12 marks)**

Higher

2001

a) Explain why opening a bed and breakfast might be a suitable business opportunity for David and Julia. **(12 marks)**

b) In addition to the details in the extract, explain what other information the bank manager would need to see in the business plan. **(12 marks)**

c) Explain how completing a business plan might help a business such as David and Julia's other than using it to show to the bank manager. **(6 marks)**

d) Why is it important for David and Julia to calculate their break-even point? **(6 marks)**

e) Discuss the possible effects of each of the above solutions on the problem and justify your choice of solution. **(12 marks)**

PEOPLE AND ORGANISATIONS

Foundation

Figure 26 WELHAM SPORTS CENTRE

Welham Sports Centre is situated next to a large secondary school in the centre of Welham. The Sports Centre is popular with young people as well as members of various sports clubs who use it for their fixtures.

The Sports Centre has a central reception area and a separate bar/café, area which is particularly busy after school and in the evenings. The Sports Centre manager and his assistant are employed full time. All other staff are employed on a part-time basis. Reception and bar/café staff receive brief training on health and safety and the information systems that are in place. This training takes approximately two hours, after which the staff are expected to be able to start work. Staff rotas are produced weekly and begin on Sunday. Staff are given the rota on the Thursday before the week starts.

Welham Sports Centre is currently experiencing the following staffing problems:

- There is a shortage of staff at weekends, when the Sports Centre is very busy.
- There is a high turnover of reception and bar/café staff.
- The hourly rate is less than that of the local supermarkets.
- Customers have complained about the rudeness and lack of interest of some of the reception staff.
- The recruitment budget is overspent.

2000

1. a) Describe how Welham Sports centre management might try to improve the motivation of its reception and bar/café staff. **(10 marks)**

   b) Explain appropriate ways for the sports centre manager to advertise for staff. **(12 marks)**

   c) Explain how the sports centre manager could select the best candidates for the reception vacancies. **(8 marks)**

Higher

2000

2. a) Describe how Welham Sports centre management might try to improve the motivation of its reception and bar/café staff. **(10 marks)**

   b) Considering the problems that the sports centre is facing, explain appropriate ways in which they could advertise for staff. **(12 marks)**

c) Explain the ways in which you think the sports centre could improve the induction training of reception and bar/café staff. **(8 marks)**

Foundation

2002

Figure 27

Below is an extract from a leaflet given to customers of Clippo, a medium-sized hairdressing salon which is advertising for a new stylist.

Your first impressions of our salon will be a friendly atmosphere matched by efficiency.

A smile will always greet you so that you feel comfortable and relaxed.

Complimentary coffee and soft drinks will put you in the mood to be pampered ...

CLIPPO
HAIR SALON

required as soon as possible

a well-qualified and experienced stylist

Phone 222 222222 for further details

---

3. a) Describe the information, other than name, address and telephone number, that Clippo would want to see on a CV. **(8 marks)**
    b) Explain suitable methods Clippo could use to select the best applicants for the job. **(12 marks)**
    c) Clippo needs to employ highly motivated staff to give the right impression to customers. Discuss how each of the following methods could help motivate its stylists and advise Clippo which should be used:
    - opportunities for further training
    - commission on sales
    - a free staff weekend in Paris. **(15 marks)**

Higher

4. a) Explain why it might be better for Clippo to require candidates to fill in an application form rather than send their CV. **(8 marks)**
    b) Explain why Clippo might use both a long and a short list to select the best applicants. **(6 marks)**
    c) Describe the best ways in which Clippo could monitor the satisfaction of its customers. **(9 marks)**